Speaking

For

Money

Speaking

For

Money

by

GORDON BURGETT

and

MIKE FRANK

COMMUNICATION UNLIMITED

P.O. Box 1001
Carpinteria, CA 93013

Also written by Gordon Burgett

The Query Book
Ten Sales From One Article Idea
How To Sell 75% of Your Freelance Writing

Second printing, 1985

Library of Congress Catalog Card Number: 84-071274

ISBN 0-910167-01-X (hardcover)

ISBN 0-910167-00-1 (paperback)

You may order single copies prepaid direct from the publisher for $9.95 (paperbound) or $12.95 (clothbound) plus $1 for postage and handling. (California residents add 6% for state sales tax). For terms on volume quantities, please contact the publisher.

Cover design by Paul Fraser.

Preface

We wrote this book for those who have something to say and want to earn a decent income from saying it.

That "something" worth saying will directly influence the size of your income. So will the way you say it, to whom it is said, and how well your presentation is promoted.

Yet the biggest determinant of your speaking income will be how badly the listener needs or wants to hear your words. Money power in speaking comes from word action: the needs those words meet, the sense of awareness they create, the powers of action they liberate.

So we have written a book that talks about the "whys" of speaking in the two most common and best-paying formats: seminars and public speeches. We offer for each the practical guidance necessary to take a subject and carry it from inception to utterance, with an eye on repeating the essence of that presentation often and for a decent income.

$1,000 a speech or a seminar? Twice that? Why not? Professional speakers do it with pleasing regularity! But not the first time out. And not if they fail to approach their speaking with the eyes, tongue, and discipline of a professional.

So that too fills these pages: how professionals do it, and how you can get to their speaking and earning plateau about as quickly as you start thinking like a professional, develop your craft, and speak with care, love, and purpose.

Our purpose in sharing this practical knowledge is straightforward: we want you to know the joy of speaking and the satisfaction of seeing in the listeners' eyes that sudden realization or welling of the spirit that comes from your words. If that isn't reward enough, we also want you to be able to give your speaking full-time attention and dedication, so we want you to be sufficiently rewarded financially to make that a reality too.

But in a book we can only write about it. You must do it. So read what we say. Apply what is appropriate and adapt it to you and your message. Then get going. Get speaking. We need to hear what you have to say!

DEDICATION

by Gordon Burgett:

Will people be offended by having a half-book dedicated to them? Alas, let me single out two groups who have made seminaring such a joy: the extended education folk throughout California who have made it possible and enjoyable, and the super people who keep showing up every time I talk, who want more out of life than they have at hand and honor me by choosing my programs as means by which they will liberate, develop, and share their ideas, skills, and knowledge with others. To both, this is a 100% dedication!

by Mike Frank:

My portion of this book is dedicated to my wonderful wife, Colleen, who has put up with my talking (for hours at a time) with speakers and aspiring speakers. We have had many a late dinner and late arrivals at a movie! My hopes are that this book will reduce some of that phone time and enable Colleen and I to share a few more personal hours a week, together, and with our terrific children, Damon and Tiffany.

ACKNOWLEDGEMENTS

by Gordon Burgett:

It is impossible to single out a few without omitting many. But in the actual preparation of this book and the mental support underlying it, I want to mention a few names: Patricia Allaback; Dr. Alan Fisher; Bud Gardner; Dr. Ira Schoenwald; and Dr. Cyril Zoerner, Jr. And of course Judy, my wife, and Shannon and Kim, my daughters. They have suffered through every page of my part of this tome!

by Mike Frank:

It would have been impossible for me to write this book if it hadn't been for the people who were my "mentors" since I got into this business in 1966. Those who are most prominent in helping me through the years, directly and indirectly, are: Hal Krause, Zig Ziglar, the late J. Douglas Edwards, Ira Hayes, Dave Yoho, and my parents, who have always given me encouragement to pursue what I wanted to do as well as being enthused about the successes and understanding about the setbacks.

TABLE OF CONTENTS

SPEECHES, by Mike Frank

Seminars

GORDON BURGETT

Gordon Burgett practices what he preaches. Speaking about "How To Set Up and Market Your Own Seminar," he offers 110 seminars a year, most at the 19 campuses of the California State University and College system, some through the University of California system, and others through community colleges.

He tells others "How To Sell 75% of Your Freelance Writing," and has been in print 900+ times. About half of those articles are travel-related, thus a seminar on "Writing Travel Articles That Sell!" (The remaining articles are about humor, sports, and general interest).

Burgett's "other" speaking led to a seminar called "Speaking For Money!" And his four books in print (plus seven others edited) are the practical know-how shared in "Before You Write That Book...."

Burgett's books were written to meet the most pressing needs of the participants attending his seminars. Querying is the difference between amateurs and professionals in the freelance writing world, so he wrote **The Query Book,** since no other book dealt specifically with this critical topic.

Ten Sales From One Article Idea confronts the second least understood marketing process, that of selling reprints and rewrites. And **How To Sell 75% of Your Freelance Writing,** a Writer's Digest Book Club top selection, addressed the entire writing/selling system in one text.

Speaking For Money unites Burgett's nuts-and-bolts explanation of how one sets up and markets their own seminar with Mike Frank's analysis of how one begins and flourishes in paid public speaking, to meet two distinct yet closely related needs in the speaking world.

Finally, he is president of Write To Sell, a publishing house, and Communication Unlimited, a consulting/speaking firm that also sells his much-sought audio cassettes about writing, speaking, and idea dissemination.

A member of both the National Speakers Association and the American Society of Journalists and Authors, Burgett previously played professional baseball; deaned at the university level; taught Portuguese, history, and communications; led an exploration up the Paushi-Yaco (Upper Amazon) River; directed CARE programs in Colombia and Ecuador; and wrote/sold comedy greeting cards. He currently leads a program called "The Idea Revolution and The Perfect Human World" and competes in triathlons.

SECTION ONE

"Getting Started"

Chapter 1

Preliminary Thoughts

It's not very important whether the annual worth of seminars is $3 billion, $5 billion, or $10 billion. You will never come close to earning that much in a lifetime of non-stop talking!

But you can make your lifetime richly rewarding in every sense by offering seminars that help others.

No star in today's educational sky shines brighter nor is any form of idea dissemination easier to enter. You need neither a degree nor a pedigree, just knowledge that others need to know; the skill and integrity to share it fully, honestly, and clearly; and the courage to do so openly on the market place.

The annual worth of seminars **is** estimated to be from three to ten billion dollars! Even better, it is growing at a spectacular rate and promises to grow even faster in the future. So if you know something, it can be shared orally, and others will pay you to know it, **seminars** is the word and **Speaking For Money** is the book.

That's a big claim on both counts. As for seminars, there's a desperate need for education in bite-sized portions. America is full of literate, bright people basically educated but woefully unprepared in the specifics. The traditional path has been to learn by doing, "figure it out," fake it, "read about it in a book," get a degree in the subject, or "ask somebody." Sometimes these work. But seminars are usually better or faster. They can be a speedy apprenticeship.

Let's say that you have some extra acres of timber: most standing, some half-fallen, the rest on the ground. You want to cut it into cords to sell. But you don't know what to cut, what is usable that's on the ground, how to replant, how to measure or store the wood, the best way to find clients, whether you should do it all yourself or hire others, any legal or insurance needs that the latter would create, or whether the preparation would make the wood too expensive to sell profitably.

Of course you might just go at it and hope that common sense would lead you to the best buck for the least amount of work. There would be some learning by doing, some "figuring it out," and a healthy whiff of faking it. You might find a recent book that answers all your questions. You could get a degree in forestry, or at least take a course (if one existed) about your specific needs. You might ask other wood sellers, trusting their responses to be 100% honest and complete. Or you could just let the wood sit there unsold.

Another approach would be to find a seminar called "How To Prepare and Sell Firewood" taught by an experienced firewood pre-parer/seller. You're clever enough that if an experienced instructor provides the facts, reasons, and aids, you can take it from there. What you really need is a bridge between basic education and specific "how-to" knowledge. That's where seminars fit in.

This book explains the "how's" of seminaring, and one will con-clude from it that the primary reason for giving seminars is financial: they can be very lucrative.

That is a valid reason. They **can** be very lucrative. But so can drug-running or loan sharking, and one would hardly write a book or brag to their granny about either. There is a much more important reason for giving seminars than blatant money-gathering, but it is not the kind of reason, sadly, to inspire most people to run the risks and work as hard as successful seminaring requires.

The reason is that by sharing information you are helping others. What you say may be the difference between a person plodding through life or being able to gather force and gain control of their destiny, with all the positive spinoffs such an affirmative change can bring to all touched by it. The words you share may be the vital link between fervent hope and reality. Or the hand that helps another over that seemingly insurmountable first incline on the way to the top of the mountain.

Everybody knows something others would benefit from knowing. That something may be an idea. Spreading that idea, sharing it with others, is called "idea dissemination." Some ideas are disseminated through articles or books, or in some other written form; others are converted into items; still others are shared orally, as in speeches or seminars.

We are alive once. Some would suggest a moral duty to share what we know with those in need. Without debating that obligation, seminaring does bring the sense of true satisfaction in seeing others benefit from using what is shared. The sharing, then, is the other reason for offering seminars.

With that reason also comes additional responsibility. What you say must be as truly useful as you can make it. It must be the truth, complete, honestly presented and fully given. Seminaring should be far more than just making a buck. If it is, the money will take care of itself.

So whether your motivation is monetary, moral, or both, Part One of **Speaking For Money** will help you set up and market your own seminar (or workshop or whatever you want to call it). No book currently on the market is this basic, yet as broad in scope. You will learn what seminars are about and why they exist, and what features are common to all seminars so that you can plug in your idea, apply the core knowledge to it, and go out and practice it. After all, before this was a book it was a seminar that was offered at least 300 times to no-nonsense, eager, demanding, loving audiences. This book does what a seminar does. It shows you how to take your knowledge, desire, and common sense and convert those into action. It is a bridge. Happy crossing!

Chapter 2

Seminars: Definitions and Kinds

Almost anybody can give a seminar. If you can speak, or even communicate in sign language, you can convey information to others, which is the essence of a seminar.

The question is whether others will pay to hear what you have to say. And since this book talks about "speaking for money," it is on that latter point -- how you can offer seminars that others will pay to hear -- that we will focus our attention.

What is a seminar?

It is a form of exchange designed to discuss or share information. Webster's **New World Dictionary** calls it a "group discussion." Others add that it is a topic- or process-centered gathering that meets once or a limited number of times. "A short, intensified course about a specific topic" most specifically defines the term as it will be used here.

A **workshop** is a kind of seminar that carries the additional connotation of physical activity as well as the transmittal of knowledge. A seminar may be sedentary; when called a workshop the implication is that the participant will be actively involved beyond just listening.

The seminar might tell how to teach the deaf to dance. A workshop would have the participants obstruct their hearing, take off their shoes, and dance to music vibrating from the floor.

A **conference** has a much wider scope, and may include both seminars and workshops. A seminar or workshop focusses on one topic and generally has one speaker. If there are several speakers, they concentrate on the same theme. A conference has a much broader theme, with many sub-topics and many speakers.

Another set of definitions

Another set of definitions comes from the National Speakers Association Leadership Workshop group, with special thanks to George Morrisey and Rosalind Newton:

SPEECH: A speech is a session of less than two hours which is designed to inspire, entertain, or stimulate ideas.

SEMINAR: A session of a half day or longer designed primarily for the transfer and discussion of information.

WORKSHOP: A structured environment for experiential learning that emphasizes discussion, exchange of ideas, demonstration of methods, and practical application of skills and principles. It actively involves participants and normally lasts a day or more.

TRAINING: A structured environment for experiential learning designed to develop specific skills in people. It actively involves participants and may last several days.

Are there various kinds of seminars?

Seminars might be defined in four ways: (1) how many parts there are to the seminar (2) why they are offered, (3) where they are given, and (4) who sponsors them.

The first category finds (a) one-part seminars and (b) two-part seminars. Yet one-part seminars don't necessarily meet once while two-part seminars often have but one part clearly defined.

For example, most one-part seminars are information-imparting. They do meet once. One attends to learn "How To Groom A Poodle." A fee is paid for four hours of knowledge, information is imparted, a poodle is groomed, and the participants are released to try their skills on other unwarned poodles.

Yet if the topic requires five hours to teach and it must be done on weekday evenings, when the longest practical class range is from 6-10 p.m., or four hours, the one-part seminar must meet twice. Another way of phrasing a "one-part" seminar would be a "single-purpose" seminar.

A two-part seminar has two purposes. **Real Estate Today** published an excellent article in their July, 1978, issue about a seminar for first-time home buyers. One element of that seminar was a three-hour presentation offered monthly to prospective first-time buyers at which the legal, financial, and procedural elements of home buying were discussed. Other than being free, that part differed little in form from the poodle-grooming seminar.

The second part, to complicate matters, required no meeting. It was to sell homes to these self-identified prospects.

The first part of a two-part seminar, then, was to inform; the second, to sell. The second part operated informally, without a time schedule or a rigid structure. A tip-off to a two-part seminar is usually the absence of a fee for the first part. Free seminars generally mean that later sales will pay the expenses of the meeting. The second part is the making of those sales.

Why seminars are offered

The second category of seminars centers on why the programs are given. Why a person, group, company, or even country would organize and offer a program to discuss or share information.

It is easy to dismiss this by saying that the "why" is money, that somebody gets paid to give information. Yet that is too superficial. True, the organizer and giver are usually paid, and in those other cases where the offering is free the offerer gains prestige and exposure from the presentation. But why the programs are given often goes deeper than the obvious rewards.

Some **are** given for the sole purpose of trading information for money. If the information is worth the cost, fine.

Others are given to sell products. "How To Cut Your Gas Consumption by 85%" might be a one-hour free demonstration of a new gizmo that attaches to the fuel pump, purchasable "that day only" at the end of the talk for $100! The distinction between the veggie slicer demos at the county fair and the full-fleshed seminar is often blade thin.

Other seminars buy good will or community acceptance. A seminar discussing land fill to a populace near such a proposed blessing serves many functions, depending upon who gives it and why. The city, in favor, might hope to replace fear with enthusiasm. Irate citizens might wish to convert fear into action. Sanitation dumpers might have other interests.

Recreation departments have a different charge. To show their service residents new ways to use their creative talents, they might sponsor seminars or workshops on "Cake Decoration,""Patio Planning and Pouring,""Hawaiian Quilting," etc.

Professional and trade organizations also offer seminars specifically directed to their members, to assist in updating or expanding their skills. In the states that require continuing education of practitioners for license renewals, seminars are also given to provide the members with new, different, additional, or "state-of-the-art" information to help them meet those licensing demands.

Businesses have internal needs that can also be met by seminars. They are often given to employees, to sales representatives, to outsiders wishing to sell items or services to the firm -- the variety is endless.

Finally, seminars provide a valuable educational expansion to colleges, universities, churches, and like organizations throughout the world.

To a university dedicated to providing core knowledge and a theoretical base for application, seminars can provide that crucial "applied" link to the outside world.

Two examples in this last case show why public seminars have mushroomed at the academic level. "How To Organize a Community Triathlon" or "Writing Fillers for Religious Magazines" carry the lessons in physical education/recreation and communications far beyond the classroom, allowing those with specific interests in those fields to learn vital information and procedural steps that will help them put their theoretical learning to immediate use.

A further thought primarily tied to the academic purpose but also evident in most of the other purposes cited: seminars allow the participant to learn much tightly-focussed material in a short period of time. Rather than having to return to a classroom at inconvenient hours for 10-15 weeks to learn the basics from which one might deduce a means of application, a seminar zeroes directly in on those means, plus the vital facts and how-to process required to put the knowledge into action. It is assumed that the listener either understands the basics or will seek those missing elements later, once the areas of specific inadequacy are known.

Where seminars are given

Where they are given is another indication of the kinds of seminars that exist. It also shows the market served.

Two general sub-categories are found here: (a) public seminars, divided into (1) public/open and (2) public/closed, and (b) private seminars, which, in turn, are divided into (1) in-house presentations and (2) licensed or customized presentations.

Public seminars are, clearly, those given in public places, such as at a college or university, a hotel, or a conference or convention center.

Public/open seminars are available to everyone. People of all backgrounds or levels of learning have access to these programs, though there may be specific restrictions against minors. Attendance is limited by interest in the topic, the fee, the time that the program is offered, and the participants' ability to reach the seminar site.

There are specific restrictions that limit attendance at a public/closed seminar. If the seminar is directed to advanced insurance brokers, for example, qualifications will keep the uninitiated away. Nursing seminars sponsored by a hospital or nursing organization will also keep the program closed to those not in nursing. The brokers or nurses needn't be from the sponsoring organization. A public announcement would let others know of the seminar's existence, but it would also note the qualifications for participation.

Private seminars are much like public/closed except that the sponsoring group will use its own facilities and/or the seminars will be directed solely to the members of its own group.

An in-house program, while primarily associated with business, could be applied to the examples just cited. The insurance and nursing groups would give the program at their own facilities, or a facility privately rented, and the seminar would be offered solely to the members of that group -- or others added to that group by invitation.

Businesses offer in-house seminars when it is more practical or economical to invite a speaker to offer a program to a specific segment of their firm -- or to like types from other firms. For example, let's imagine that a small firm is having difficulty with its memo writing. Everybody does them differently: some write endless, prosaic memos; some limit complicated communiques to three words; others won't write them at all; and still others write them unintelligibly.

A person is hired who is knowledgeable about memo writing to offer a three-hour morning seminar to the entire firm, president to pick-up boy. It is offered "in-house." The company provides the location, promotion, supplies, support, and a fee to the seminar-giver. The latter provides himself, a seminar, and all needed audio-visual supplies, plus a model workbook and examples for the firm to duplicate and provide the day of the presentation.

Incidentally, if the memo mess was confined, say, to shipping, and this was a problem also suffered by other nearby firms, those firms might pool their efforts and provide an "in-house" program at one of the plants for all of the shipping staffs at the same time, splitting the costs proportionally.

A licensed seminar is usually one that is pre-packaged and can be given at a company when needed. The package is usually bought or rented on a licensee arrangement, and often includes workbooks, software, video or audio cassettes, or even live speakers or coordinators. Continuing the above example, a memo-writing seminar might consist of an introductory video cassette followed by a software program where the individual can practice writing memos against a format. That would be "packaged" and available on an occasional basis or rented or bought for continual use.

It is estimated that half of the money in seminars is linked to customized presentations. To the uninitiated they are the submerged part of the iceberg. They are also the hardest for the newcomer to book.

Customized presentations are tailor-made to the needs of larger groups or companies. Again, to extend our example to show how it would apply at this level of seminar, a giant firm knows that its field workers have trouble with memo writing. Needs, directions, and ideas aren't working their way upward, and too much money is being lost on garbled or misunderstood information. Because much of the information at that level uses the same terms and concepts, it could be simplified and an easy-to-use format could be adapted that would both clarify and simplify.

So the training division turns to a person experienced in this field for consultation. He proposes an 8-step program: (1) a look at the memos now being written to see where improvement is needed and how the writing could be clarified and simplified for all, (2) the development of a two-hour workshop to be given on site to all field workers, which in turn would require (3) the creation of a uniform presentation, with audio-visual tools, workbooks, and a one-page guide sheet for the employees to keep, for reference. The consultant would (4) offer this workshop to the training staff. The presentation would be modified, if needed, and (5) the consultant or the training staff would deliver it to the field crew supervisors who, in turn, (6) would present the workshop to the field workers. An evaluation (7) would follow, and some months or a year later (8) a review of the process would be made, for any modifications or alterations necessary.

There are as many variations of the above example as there are large firms and differing needs, but some common points can be made: customized seminars are usually built around an in-house presentation designed by the seminar-giver for the purpose of being repeated on a regular basis by others within that firm. The seminar-giver is usually brought in as a consultant, and in addition to designing the basic seminar the consultant usually oversees the training of its presenters as well as devises a tool to measure the program's effectiveness.

Why would a large firm prefer a customized seminar to bringing in one person to offer an in-house program as needed? Because it is far less expensive to pay its own employees to offer a program, because the need may be so widespread or immediate it would be impossible or impractical to have one person try to meet it, or because the firm doesn't want to be that dependent on outside assistance.

Who sponsors seminars?

The fourth means of identifying seminars is by who sponsors them. Eight such seminar sponsors are evident:

(1) self-sponsored
(2) self-sponsored but aligned with another group or organization for mutual benefit
(3) academic
(4) recreational
(5) professional association
(6) trade association
(7) business
(8) other

A few of these need additional explanation. In the second example it is possible for an individual or company offering self-sponsored programs to align themselves with another group for mutual benefit. Let's say that a person offering a seminar to train baseball umpires usually gives his program through colleges, (3) above, and sometimes on his own (1) where the college is too far from those eager to learn the rudiments of umpiring.

But in Slugville there is an active Baseball Boosters Club, a fully established non-profit organization, and it is eager to get more fathers and even older players involved in umpiring. So there the person strikes a deal with the Boosters. He will offer them his program at a reduced rate if they will find a location for him to use free, he can use their name for sponsorship, and he can put their "P.S.A." (public service announcement) number on his press releases. Everybody wins. The Boosters get his priceless services at a lower price while he avoids a room rental, gets tacit approval by their sponsorship, and greatly enhances the chances of his promotional material being used with the P.S.A. classification on it.

The business (7) category is all-inclusive: public seminars to sell products, good will seminars to influence a community, in-house programs, licensed or customized offerings, and so on. The other (8) category is likewise all-inclusive. It includes anything overlooked in the first seven!

Chapter 3

Finding a Subject

"How do you find a subject for a seminar?"

That's an easy question to answer. Find a need, then design a seminar that meets or satisfies that need.

If that sounds too simple, look at seminar titles. Then ask why people pay to attend them. They do so because they benefit from those seminars. Individuals pay and attend to learn new skills to advance their careers, to qualify them for better positions, to find more happiness or less distress, to improve their tennis games, to save money when buying a personal computer.... Companies send employees to seminars for the same reason: the company somehow benefits.

Benefits are the results of confronting and solving problems or of meeting needs. Some problems or needs are urgent, others are anticipated. Some are illusory; others are superficial. Some people attend seminars because they are bored and want to meet new people or fill empty hours. Some want to associate with others like themselves and suspect that at a seminar they will at least find folks with similar interests. Others attend to find clients among the audience to whom they can sell their products or services. Those too are needs.

The more basic the need, the more likely your seminar is to attract registrants. If a person feels that need once a week, he may well attend to get it met. But if he feels it daily, a team of horses may not be able to pull him away. So you might best focus on those most commonly felt needs that lend themselves to seminar solution.

Some do not. Raging anxiety might be an ugly, all-hour's companion but a seminar won't cure it. A toothache is an urgent need not met by a seminar. The list of needs not suitable to seminar solution is long.

But the list of topics that do lend themselves well to seminars is also long. Scores of useful, needed seminars can be devised around such basic concerns as health, happiness, beauty, conservation, security, prosperity, success, laughter, time use, creativity, sexual happiness, achievement, relaxation, travel, and hundreds more subjects that are important to people.

Many of those topics are also important to business. But so is money, and most of the seminars commonly offered to business and industry are clearly linked to the latter: how to cut losses, how to increase sales, how to increase productivity, how to lift morale, how to instill eternal dedication to the product or the boss....

So for starters you must find a need you wish to meet with your seminar. Write that need, or many needs, on a sheet of paper. Easy, isn't it?

An important question

One presumes that a purpose of your offering seminars is to earn money. There are other purposes, of course, but sooner or later seminar-givers want to be compensated for their efforts. That provokes a crucial question, "If you give a seminar will anybody pay to hear it?"

That is, will anybody dress up and hire a babysitter and miss the lodge meeting or the movie on HBO to hear you speak? You expect your audience to do all that -- and to cheer when you're done! Or you want some tight-fisted boss to bring you in talk to' his workers when they otherwise would be slaving at their punch presses making him money.

So let's ask it again: "If you give a seminar will anybody pay to hear it?"

Until you can answer a resounding "you bet!" -- and add that they'd be damn fools **not** to want to hear it at any cost, -- you're not ready yet.

A guideline that will help

Now that you have a sheet of paper with a topic or topics on it and a question that you must affirmatively answer before you offer your program to humans, let's add a one-sentence guideline that will help you further refine your search for the right topic or topics. It says:

"Sell hard-to-find but easy-to-apply information to participants who perceive that it will meet their needs."

Lasting and lucrative success seems to lie in the application of those words. The two key elements are **information** and **perception.**

The **information** you sell to others through a seminar should be that which they need to know but can't readily acquire or won't. In either case you must show them that it is financially more sensible to let you explain it, in gathered form, than for them to spend their time gathering it themselves.

Some information is spread out thinly and is tediously collected or hard to find for the novice. Other information comes from experience and/or interviews that people haven't the time or accessibility to obtain. So you do the digging and sell the results.

Or it is information they would benefit from knowing but isn't, in their opinion, worth the extra effort. Often they can function without knowing more than the basics, albeit at a less informed level. So you gather the additional knowledge, tell them how they would benefit even more from knowing it, and sell it in a seminar format.

A perfect example of why it is economically sensible to get information in seminar form is the very material about seminars you are reading in this book, which is also offered at a seminar. Every fact included is findable by others, if they dig persistently and widely enough. Only the writer's experience is not readily accessible, but other seminar-givers would surely offer similar comments. It simply makes sense to learn it in one place at a four-hour sitting rather than spending months putting it together fact by fact. The economy of time and labor are as much selling tools of a seminar as the quality of the material and the manner of presentation.

There is more to information than just finding it, though. To be presented as a seminar that information must be reordered in a logical and easily comprehensible fashion, which in turn usually requires that it be condensed. We will discuss seminar preparation and organization later, but fundamental to all is that there be sufficient, accurate material for an honest presentation.

The second variable in this one-sentence guide is **perception.** To get a person to pay to attend your seminar he must perceive both a need and the seminar as a way to meet that need. The same for companies paying for their employees to hear your words: what need can you meet that will justify the fee and lost time on the job?

Let's say that your seminar helps participants raise their self-esteem. A good topic. There's no shortage of people with low self-esteem, and much loss of achievement and happiness because of it. But getting them to show up at your seminar can be a major accomplishment. Not that they disagree with what you're doing. They just won't come **because they're not worthy.** They have low self-esteem! They don't perceive the seminar as being for them. It's for better people, those worth helping!

(The solution here is in the promotion, the title, and the description. Your advertising, for example, might say in large letters "IS THIS HOW YOU'D LIKE TO BE?" followed by a description of an active, popular person full of self-esteem. The next panel would ask "IS THIS HOW YOU ARE?" The description is of a person with low self-esteem, with all the earmarks of that state. The third panel would say "THEN YOU MUST ATTEND THIS SEMINAR!" with every detail one needs to know to attend: place, time, length, cost, who to contact, etc. Where there is no perception, you must provide it. The same is true if there is perception but no motivation.)

So information and perception must be key elements in selecting, then promoting, topics for successful seminars. See if these elements and the one-sentence guide aren't present in every seminar you study or attend. Then make certain they are evident in your own.

Listing the needs and benefits

You already have a topic or topics listed on your paper, and that number will increase as you further define and develop your seminar. Each time you encounter a topic you must subject it to the same exercise. Write beside or below it NEED(S) and BENEFIT(S).

The need(s) will be those that will be met in some way by taking your seminar. The benefit(s) will be those received by the person or company paying the fee to attend.

This exercise is far more than game-playing. If you can't find a need or a benefit, you don't have a proper topic for a seminar. The more of each that you find, and the more they relate to one's central life drives, the better your chances are of having a topic that will be profitable.

You will also need this list when you write the seminar's description and title, when you book your program through or with a sponsor, and when you prepare promotional material. The list is truly gilded. It is the single best indication of topics that should succeed, markets that will seek your seminar, and roll-out products and services that can expand your efforts and income manifoldly.

Defining the seminar's purpose

Now take the "best" topic on your paper, with its needs/benefits list, and ask what the purpose of that seminar would be.

Your topic might be advertising for pizza parlors, since your background is in advertising and you see a dozen ways that pizza parlors could increase their sales by better promotion. The need is to increase the sales of pizza and other food items for the parlors -- a need all would recognize and pay to have met. The benefits would be more income for the parlors, more jobs or hours for employees, sales prices for customers, more promotion money for the various media, and greater tax revenue for the city and state.

With that defined you should state the purpose of your seminar in one sentence. It might be "The purpose of my seminar is to increase the sale of pizza and other food items at pizza parlors through better and more advertising."

Then take that sentence and switch it into a working question: "How can pizza parlors increase their sale of pizza and other foods through better and more advertising?" From that working question comes the secondary questions that must be answered at the seminar. The working question or the statement of purpose also provides the core of your promotional material, since that purpose provides the framework from which the benefits come.

The secondary questions show you the kind of information you will need to know before you present your program. They will let you evaluate your idea against other seminars already being given to see how much of your material is included in their presentations. And it will provide an organizational structure to use when writing a seminar description.

For example, secondary questions from the statement of purpose above might be:

(1) How much of an increase in pizza and other food sales could come from better and more advertising?
(2) What kind of advertising are you talking about?
(3) What is "better" advertising? Against what standard?
(4) How much more advertising would be required?
(5) Would this require new personnel? Would the skills needed to increase and improve the advertising be taught at the seminar?
(6) How much of a net income increase could the parlors expect from greater sales after they pay for better and more advertising?

The actual seminar would include more information than the answers to these and the working question, of course, but these would be the core of what the participant expects to hear. Thus this core should be central to your title, description, research, and promotion.

The topic is where you start. The guideline statement provides a form of orientation and evaluation. The needs/benefits list shows why others will register, and the working question, and the secondary questions that come from it or the statement of purpose, suggest the core of the material to be covered.

Later you will find markets and sponsors, but first let's look at a key element in planning, the feasibility study.

Chapter 4

Feasibility Study

Now that you have a topic in mind, you must do some checking to see if it is (1) feasible to market that topic, and (2) feasible to present a seminar about it. For obvious reasons this will be your "feasibility study."

A seminar called "How To Decipher Chibchan Writing" sounds properly academic and perfectly appropriate but for two things: it is unmarketable and it is impossible to prepare. Chibcha Indians, living in what we now know as Colombia, had no writing. And anybody interested enough to take this rather esoteric offering would know that and wouldn't sign up.

Few topics will be so ideally unsuited to a seminar. Most are based on facts and needs that you perceive, and seem simple enough to prepare once you have done the necessary research. Still, a few dollars and a few hours spent checking both those facts and assumptions can save hundreds, even thousands, of dollars later.

As to marketability, the main reason that others would not pay to attend a seminar is (1) there are other seminars about the same or a closely related subject, (2) they can get the same information cheaper, faster, or better some other way, (3) they don't believe that the seminar will help them, (4) they don't care enough about the topic to want to give up time and money to attend.

Check and see if there are other seminars in this field. Don't panic if there are many; worry if there are too few. Ask why nobody or just one brave soul or two is speaking about this subject. Is the subject so new that you are on the front edge of competition? Are (2), (3), or (4) above the answer? Or aren't others as perceptive as you in seeing a need and figuring out a way to market it?

Finding Other Seminars

How do you find seminars that are already being offered? Some are clamoring to be known; others take considerable digging.

Academic institutions and recreational organizations usually advertise their programs through catalogs or bulletins. To receive the latest copy as well to be added to their mailing lists, simply call their offices and ask.

If you are a professional or practicing a trade you may already belong to an organization offering seminars. If not, check to see if those groups have such programs and if they will mail appropriate information to you as it becomes available. Trade and professional newspapers, newsletters, and journals are excellent sources for seminar advertising as well.

Seminar-giving organizations, such as the American Management Association or Learning Resources, will gladly add you to their mailing. ASTD members are well versed on such organizations. And close attention to the ads in big city newspapers will reveal many mass market seminars.

A more tedious but ultimately far more informative way is to concentrate on one market. For example, let's say that you want to offer seminars to electronics firms with from 30-150 employees. You might directly contact some firms at either end of that range, explaining precisely what you want to do, gently extoll the virtues of your coming program, and ask if it would be possible to review all of the flyers about seminars, workshops, and conferences that they receive in an average month.

The approach makes so much sense and would require so little work on their part -- either pulling a file or saving the items in a box for a month -- that to your surprise companies might well agree to help you out. Resistance might be met by promising a half-price program once you get going. Or a lunch for the lucky secretary in charge of your project.

You will not only find out the kind of competition you will be facing, you will see how that competition presents itself. You will know the graphics required, the fees asked, what topics others perceive as important, how the flyers are addressed, and whether somebody else is hustling the same kind of program you want to offer.

The last, obvious way is simply to ask others in that field about seminars that are being given and how you can get more details.

Attending Those Seminars

Now that you know your seminar competition, attend their seminars! Nothing will teach you more about how to give seminars than seeing how others give theirs. Even awful presentations will teach you much; excellent programs will show you the level of competence you must equal or surpass.

Do you open yourself to some future suit by having your name on their roster sheet? Hardly. Seminars aren't copyrighted, though the workbooks may be. Words personally delivered can no more be protected than a person can put a fence around an idea. An analogy: one person writes an article about beet growing. That doesn't prevent anybody else from also writing about beet growing -- just so they don't use the same words in the same order as the first person! The same holds true for seminars.

Show up an hour ahead of the scheduled time. Apologize for being early, quietly take a seat, and unobtrusively observe everything the other person does. Unless the speaker talks to you, just be quiet and watch. See how the person cleans and sets up the room, displays visuals, organizes the book or tape display, prepares handouts, greets folks, and glides into the opening remarks. A few minutes of post-seminar observation will likewise pay big dividends later. Observe a veteran do what you must soon do. See how that person saves time and motion while creating the proper setting for the talk.

After the seminar, note the areas that weren't well covered, other topics that came to mind while you listened, spinoff or follow-up seminars that might be needed. Review the workbook and all handouts: do they suggest ways that you could compete against or around this seminar? Could you market your program better? Had an obvious audience been overlooked?

How else can a person get the same information?

Seminars are generally an economical and enjoyable way to learn. The speaker studies the field, gathers the facts and opinions, puts the results in an easily digestible format, supplements that with printed and audio-visual material, and presents it in an pleasant way.

Still, if the same material is available in a 1500-word article or on a few sheets of paper, who would spend hours and dollars to attend your seminar? Other forms of idea dissemination are less threatening to seminaring. Full books take too long to read, speeches are generally shorter and less conducive to note-taking or retention, and audio-cassettes are usually heard in a car or where notes are hard to take. Video-cassettes will be in direct competition soon, though for most the technology and machinery are still a few years off.

There is one aspect of seminaring that is hard to replace: the physical gathering of people with similar interests or needs. Writers go to seminars to meet other writers, dentists to meet other dentists, and so on. This might even be mentioned in your promotion.

So one basic question you must answer before investing heavily in a seminar: "How else can this information be found?" If providing it at a seminar makes the most sense, or will appeal to most of the people in that field, you have another green light!

People must believe that the seminar will help them!

If you offered a seminar called "How To Earn a Billion Dollars Translating Basque Movie Scripts," you'd have an empty house. Not that the lure isn't large enough -- only the rare Basque knows there are no movies in his tongue. People just won't register because they know that they can't read Basque.

Seminars far less obviously misnamed will still fail to convince people to register because they don't believe that they will benefit. They don't want to look or feel foolish so they won't risk the time and fee.

Tell a person that you can make him a million dollars with IRA's and he will rub his hands with greedy gratitude. But tell him that he can make a million dollars by attending your seminar and he probably won't be there. Those attuned to finance, conversant in investments, and daring -- they will attend. But the average person will hold back.

It's feasible to market a seminar if you can somehow make the reader believe. Believe that what you say is true, that the benefits will in fact be his, that he has the ability and skills to do what is required to receive them, that he won't look foolish or stupid in the process, and that he won't be laughed at just for attending.

The seminar participant must care

It takes time and money to attend a seminar, and of the two time is usually the most reluctantly yielded. Given their druthers most people would fill every hour their own ways, justifying idle time with the same vigor they justify their most productive moments.

So if you are to get some of that time you must show people why it is more important to attend your seminar, cloaked as it is by the dangers and uncertainties of the unknown, than not to attend. You must give them a reason; they must care enough about your subject to decide to alter their usual way of doing things.

That care needn't be of a loving nature. Telling people "How To Detoxify Your Water" is a crucial, albeit negative, issue of pressing importance if their water is bubbling with toxins -- and they are thirsty!

You usually convince people to attend your seminar by telling them what they will get if they do -- benefits, hope, laughter, a spouse, etc. -- or what they will get if they don't -- a social disease, bankruptcy, children who can't read, a spouse, etc. You must make them care enough to register, pay, and attend.

Is it feasible to present the seminar?

A seminar could be marketable but impossible to prepare or present.

The material may be so complex that it doesn't lend itself to oral presentation. Forms of mathematics, economics, and electronics come to mind where the material is best seen in written or symbolic form. To do it right you'd need three blackboards or three projection screens, lots of pointing, and too little light for notetaking.

Or the subject may be too lengthy or complex for a seminar, which generally run from three to eight hours long. You simply cannot teach Portuguese, for example, in one seminar. Or how to play the oboe, "Chemistry from A to Z," or how to spell.

Sometimes the setting is the difficulty. Hiking along the Andes defies seminar packaging. Antigravitational capsule coordination, base stealing, and bat capturing likewise lend themselves better to other educational formats.

You get the idea. Seminars usually come in one of three forms: the perfect length (which means the material has been artfully trimmed and packaged to the hours available), an overview (centering on the critical parts of a greater body of information), or a microview (focussing on one aspect of the subject, like "How to Install a Drive Shaft" from the whole of repairing a car). Yours must do the same.

The next step, then, presuming that your topic is both marketable and presentable, is to write a description.

Chapter 5

Description

Once you have a topic, a working question, secondary questions, and the needs/benefits determined, and you feel that your idea is feasible to prepare and market, you must compose a full written description of the seminar.

Why? To define the purpose of the presentation precisely, so you can explain how you will achieve that purpose in the hours alloted. Much or all of the description will appear in print, so those contemplating registration will also know of your intention and how you propose to realize it. And much of it will be the core of your promotional copy.

Thus it is imperative that the description be comprehensive, concise, and appealing. From it will come the title. The two, title and description, are the cover to your book, figuratively: they convince the interested to register. So once the title, like a headline, catches their interest, the description, like the article, must explain and reinforce it. Unlike an article, it must also convince.

Spend time writing your description. Write it in segments, rewrite it, and rewrite it again, editing and moving pieces around and editing once more until every word, every phrase is exact, honest, and clearly understandable.

Journalistic techniques help. Keep paragraphs to a sentence or two, three maximum -- and if three, all very short. Start with a lead, or opening paragraph, that feeds from the title and makes one want to read more. It would likely include the key benefits of attending the seminar or explain why the reader can do what the seminar proposes.

The second or third paragraph often lists the benefits to the participant or explains the steps to be taken at the presentation, a sort of schedule in summary form. These are usually written in list form, in

Seminar Description Sheet

DESCRIPTION

How To Set Up and Market Your Own Seminar

Want to earn $1000 a day -- or a second income -- selling what you know to others? Or share knowledge with clients or prospective customers at free, informative, image-enhancing gatherings? Seminars and workshops are the magic words sweeping America. In four hours you will learn the essential ingredients of seminar/workshop success:

* how to give your first seminar without risk and virtually no cost

* what promotional strategies work

* what four key questions seminar-/workshop-givers must be able to answer

* why topic definition and title choice are the single most important ingredients of success

* how to determine fee, length, location, and day/hour

A workbook, free to seminar participants, includes an organizational calendar, a current bibliography, a sample news release, and a model evaluation form, plus sections about publicity, mailing lists, locations, flyer/brochure preparation, budget, content and organization, and how to get scheduled at colleges and universities.

Even more, Gordon Burgett, a member of the National Speakers Association who offers 110 seminars a year, will explain what he is doing as he does it, tying together form and content in one fact-packed program designed to provide you with the basic information and tools needed to get you speaking (and banking) quickly, confidently, and permanently.

SEMINAR LENGTH: 4 hours
MINIMUM COST: $40, including workbook

Gordon Burgett
537 Arbol Verde St.
Carpinteria, CA 93013
(805) 684-2469
Soc. Sec. #000-00-0000

short sentences, phrases, or a few words each. Instead of having numbers before each item, a circle (the letter "o" in your typewriter) or a
star (*) precede each listing, all indented with a space between each
line.

This summary listing is very important. The reader will see the
title first, will jump to the summary listing, then, if interested, will
read the whole description, starting with the lead, the listing again
(skimmed) and the short paragraphs that follow. So you must help the
reader by keeping the copy flowing sensibly, using words the reader will
know, and showing, in print, the same clarity and ease of communication you plan to carry over into your seminar.

When you are putting the description together, read descriptions
of other seminars. Focus on those that appeal to you. What caught your
attention? Why do those descriptions, or write-ups, have more pull?
Use the same techniques that make them excell.

The more material you have to work with, initially, the easier it
will be to write the description and later promotional releases. So spend
time with the working and secondary questions, with tentative combinations and schedules, with needs and benefits lists, with a thesaurus
and dictionary seeking the best terms and easily understood synonyms,
with different ways of making the same facts sound interesting.

Talk about the things that would motivate a potential registrant
to sign up and attend. Would he expect to make' money from your
message? Then tell how that is possible, with examples (if available and
verifiable). Does he expect to learn the essentials to organize his own
shop, or program, or wardrobe by color? Then promise that, and give
the steps you will discuss to make it a reality.

Particularly beguiling are phrases like "the four things every
robot repairman needs to know to succeed" or "the keys to robot repair
riches...." The reader interested in robot repair can hardly afford **not**
to be in your audience! But be sure that those "things" or "keys" are
legitimate and based on more than guesswork or supposition.

How do these descriptions vary for the different forms of seminars?

Self-sponsored: Your description will be the heart of your promotion -- the core of your brochures and your advertising. Remember, it
must be full of benefits and clear as to what you will do and why the
person should attend. Help the reader justify spending the registration
fee by indicating that the seminar will offer information unavailable
elsewhere.

Academic: The description will be your chief selling tool at colleges and universities, when accompanied by your resume or list of credentials for offering the seminar in question. It will also be the core of your listing in the bulletins distributed to extended education clientele. So it must be written both to sell you to a director, for booking, and to sell the seminar to potential registrants.

The description example that follows is one sent to book and publicize a seminar at many of the state universities in California. It is a good length for bulletins. It also tells, below the line, other vital facts needed by the various extended education directors: the length of the seminar, its cost (and what is included for that cost beyond the seminar itself), the name and address of the seminar-giver, a phone for contact, and the social security number (altered here).

In-house: The description must be written from a different perspective: the purpose must be oriented to why the business would sponsor the seminar and what results would accrue to that business, and secondarily to the participants who attend. The writing must be more objective, less hyped. Your name (or company name) and address/phone will be included but length and cost will be left off, to be settled by negotiation. One must also be careful not to give too many details about the content or process lest a trainer at the company decide that, knowing precisely what you are going to do and how, he can save money, gather up some facts, and do the same thing himself.

Chapter 6

Title

A title is the single most important selling tool of a seminar. If the title doesn't make sense, if it doesn't make its reader want to reap the benefits or at least know more about the subject, that person will pick a different seminar -- or none at all.

So title selection should take time and be based on something more than whim or back-pocket logic.

Picking a title should follow the gathering and writing of a description because then you know what you are titling. You know why your seminar exists, what it's to do, and how it will do it. With a good description and a title to sell it, all that separates you from profit paradise are the magic words, your dynamic presentation, and an audience!

Go back to the working question and see if it doesn't suggest some titles. State the purpose in different ways. Play with words. Make a list of a dozen or more titles -- just so each promises what your seminar does.

Consider using one or some of these terms said to include the most persuasive words in the English language: new, how to, save, discover, safety, health, you, guarantee, love, easy, money, proven, free, and results. Particularly the words "you," "how to," and "free."

Then integrate action verbs to create selling copy. Don't try to impress others with polysyllabic tongue-twisters known only to you and Webster. The title should move the listener to action, not to the dictionary!

The strongest word in the title will be the first noun or verb; the second most remembered will be the last word. Weak lead words will push that thrust to the words that follow. For example, "How To **Set Up** and **Market** Your Own **Seminar**" will primarily emphasize "set up" (and "market" because of the conjunction), with secondary emphasis on "seminar" -- which are precisely the words the seminar-giver wants you to remember. But "How **You** Can Set Up and Market Your Own **Seminar**" stesses the wrong thing. (Don't underline words in your titles. That is done here to show the stressed words.)

Gerunds will switch the emphasis to the word that follows, so be certain that is your intention. "Writing **Travel** Articles That **Sell**!" works well because the intention is to emphasize "travel" articles, rather than other kinds of articles, and "sell." But "Writing **Any** Articles So They Will **Sell**" has the emphasis all wrong and is needlessly wordy. "Writing **Articles** That **Sell**!" is far better in the latter case.

Don't worry about copyrighting your title: it can't be done. Just try to find a title that is short, catchy, accurate, and appropriate. Short because it is easier to remember a few words than many. If you use more than six words, generally, your title must be typeset in two lines (a "double-decker"). It's simply harder for two lines to attract as well as one -- or to be as well remembered.

"Catchy" is, in itself, a catchy word: it catches your attention for being concise and a bit clever. A catchy word sounds good; a catchy title has a sharp ring to it. But never sacrifice accuracy and appropriateness for it. If your title isn't accurate -- if you promise "A" and in truth you will be talking about "B" -- you are the one who will pay. You must face the audience every minute of every hour, dodging hostility at its having been lured with false bait. Appropriateness refers more to tone. If your seminar is stiff and formal, the title shouldn't be folksy or loose. You'll attract whittlers to the coming-out ball.

Try your list of a dozen or more titles on lots of people. (If it's a seminar for unicorn hunters, be sure some of those people are unicorn hunters.) Have them pick **the best,** then a couple of second bests. Pay attention to the consensus: for as many reasons as there are people they will tend to gravitate toward the same titles. Consider those choices seriously.

But make a choice. You can abort the best seminar by never giving it a name. Pick a title and stick with it. Seminars cultivate followers who want to recommend it to friends, so you change titles later at some peril. But if a title doesn't attract listeners after a well-promoted try or two, look for a better title -- or topic.

Remember, nothing will help sell a seminar more than its title. A title is like a person's name. You'd think twice before calling yourself Glyngk Stlaxk. Exercise the same care with your seminar.

How might you look differently at titles in each category?

Self-sponsored: As stated above, the title pulls -- or it doesn't. If it doesn't, your seminar will indeed be self-sponsored. You will pay for the empty chairs.

Academic: The only difference is that the more theoretical the university is in definition and practice the more likely it will be to want to reword your seminar title, eliminating terms that suggest selling, money, profits, etc. It may also edit your write-up along the same line. So you must either have an agreement in advance that neither the title nor description will be changed or you must, at the least, be consulted before any such changes are made. It may be too late to cancel the presentation that semester or quarter, but if the sales appeal is edited out, you may be forced to look elsewhere for a sponsor with more practical sense the next time around.

In-house: Here the title, like the description, must be written to match the reason that the business is booking you. It needn't be overly flamboyant since you don't have to attract participants through your title. It must clearly state what will happen at the presentation or why it is being given. The same seminar will often have different titles when given publically and in-house. The latter will be more descriptive, less benefit-oriented.

Chapter 7

Market Identification

While you were working on a description and title you must have had somebody in mind to attend. Now you must concentrate on clearly identifying those somebodys so your promotional costs aren't more than you could earn from registrations.

It's possible to have a super idea, fetching title, compelling description, and no seminar because drawing an audience would cost you more, prorated, than folks would pay to hear you speak. The financial feasibility of seminaring, then -- assuming that you have a salable topic, title, and description -- comes from market targeting and selecting the most appropriate way to reach the "best" market(s).

To begin that market identification, list every type of person, vocation, hobby, or group that would benefit from attending your seminar. Not that would just "be interested" -- interest alone won't open many wallets. Who would benefit sufficiently to register, pay, travel to and fro, sit attentively, and substitute the time otherwise spent on other activities or pastimes? People attend seminars to receive benefits.

Once you have compiled a list of beneficiaries, put a number "1" by that person or group most benefitted, a "2" by the second most benefitted, a "3" by the next, and just keep the rest in mind. The numbers will indicate where your budget for promotion will be spent. Most of it will be spent on "1"; most of the rest on "2", and what's left on "3."

Why? Because the probability of attendance is directly proportional to the benefits perceived. So you will devote your limited promotional funds to those people where your chances of registrations are the best. The others may hear of the program through free promotions or word-of-mouth. We'll discuss promotion later. Now you must put the list of those most likely to attend in a priority order with the most likely first, in decreasing likelihood.

At this point you have completed your initial market identification. You have pursued a singular path from idea to feasibility study through a needs/benefits analysis to a description and title. And now you have compiled a list, in order, of those most likely to attend.

You may be ready to select the kind of sponsorship, and then seek sponsors, which are the final preparatory steps prior to writing the actual seminar, setting it up, and giving it. If so, you may wish to skip the next section.

Yet most seminars start with one idea and one market in mind, and by the time the organizer has reached this stage he sees ten ways the topic could be given, twenty modifications, and a huge question: do I continue with my original description and title, and save the spinoffs until later, or do I go back, look into related seminars more closely now, and reconsider which would in fact be the most sensible first seminar, and which of the others, if any, are worthy of pursuit quickly and with equal vigor?

Perhaps a section about "market expansion" would be useful before zeroing in on a "first" seminar to which you will give total attention during its launching.

Chapter 8

Market Expansion

Some beneficiaries -- potential attendants -- will come immediately to mind. Others may be suggested by where similar seminars are normally offered or where there is an increase in the need that your program addresses. You may offer a "How To Prepare a Job Resume" seminar through adult education and at a local university. You read that a nearby plant will close down in three months. Guess who will need job resumes? Or see a similar seminar being given for graduating doctors. So why not a specific resume-writing program for graduating nurses, dentists, art majors, chemists, etc.?

Sometimes it's as easy as matching the topic to the kinds of people. You want to offer a seminar about computer use. The program that you would offer a family ("How To Pick the Perfect Home Computer for Your Family") is far different from a seminar for optometrists ("Picking the Right Computer for Today's Optometrist"). In all cases the market dictates the seminar best suited to its needs.

Confusing? A confusion of riches. You began with one idea and prepared a list of the folks most likely to attend a seminar based on that idea. Yet as you looked more closely, the idea bred related, seminar-yielding ideas. And, in compiling a list of those most likely to attend your original seminar, you saw that by altering the topic some you could give a specific seminar to each of the kinds of people on your first list. You wound up with 20 possible seminars!

Examples of this blissful dilemma. You decide to offer a seminar called "How To Write Magazine Articles That Sell," and you develop a list of the kinds of people most likely to attend: writers, English/communications majors, newspaper writers, retirement folk, professionals or academics for their respective journals, and just plain people "who've always wanted to be in print." A rather vague list.

The more you think about it, the more you wonder whether you couldn't also give seminars about your other areas of expertise. These you might tentatively title "Trade Magazine Article Writing," "Writing Travel Articles That Sell," "Sports Writing That Pays," and "Writing Greeting Cards That Sell." Each seminar would have its own list of possible attendants.

Then you review the list of less likely participants at your original seminar, those with the (3) priority number in "Market Identification" or no number at all, to see if you couldn't tailor-make different seminars that would appeal more specifically to them. You could offer "Retirees: How To Get Into Print Often and Profitably." You you might offer "Academics: How To Write For the Popular Market" or even "How To Crack Into Those Academic Journals."

Or you might look at your expanded list of potential seminars and your list of lower priority folk to come up with still other combinations, like "Nurses: How To Write For Publication." A seminar that would combine your topics of writing, selling, and targetting to both the trade and professional magazines.

Then again you might see where writing itself is in need of help. One spot comes immediately to mind: our previous example, memo writing! So why not an in-house "Proper Memo Writing" seminar?

You'll notice that we've worked from a general topic (for anybody interested in writing for publication) to specific ones (for nurses and about memos). You can also think from the specific to the general; or laterally, to other general topics or to other specific markets.

Let's focus on these three choices later: "How To Write Magazine Articles That Sell," "Nurses: How To Write For Publication," and "Proper Memo Writing." On the surface the first seems to be a big moneymaker; the seminar for nurses, small change; and the third, anywhere from nothing to a windfall, if given to a large corporation.

But you can't bank on guesswork. Nor do you have to. You can remove most of the logic of whim and wish by asking some straightforward questions, then picking the best form of sponsorship before investing much hard cash.

So for now, if you found additional seminars you want to offer, zero in on one, two, three, even four more. Take each through the steps we have previously discussed: topic definition, feasibility study, needs/benefits analysis, description, title, and initial market identity. Later you will rank the seminars in a priority order for pursuit and find sponsors for them. Now let's ask the four questions that will help you select the best sponsor.

Chapter 9

Sponsorship Selection

By now you've got one or several seminars defined, titled, and even peopled on paper. That costs nothing and is full of promise. But soon you're going to have to spend actual money (beyond the costs of the feasibility study), so you'd best figure out how to maximize your income and minimize your outflow and risk before you deal in true tender.

Right now you're a bit like a lass all gussied up for the ball. Lots of planning and imaginary dancing, powdered and primped, full of expectations. But you have no invitation! Since you didn't get a sponsor in advance, to have the fun you'll have to use your wits. In seminar terms, that's self-sponsoring, and in either terms, it's just plain risky!

Not that self-sponsoring in seminaring is bad. It can be the most lucrative path -- or it can be the most costly. So you will want to consider all three general forms of sponsorship: self-sponsored, co-sponsored (where you share the risks and the income with another group or person), or totally sponsored (where you are paid to provide your services). The risk progressively decreases, but so does the chance for a windfall.

The answers to four questions will help you decide which of the forms of sponsorship will be most appropriate for you:

(1) Where would the registrant expect to attend the seminar?

(2) How much would that registrant expect to pay to attend?

(3) What are the most effective means of identifying and contacting the potential top priority registrants for this seminar?

(4) How much does it cost, per potential registrant, to make that contact?

Let's subject our three writing seminars to these questions so we can see how a similar topic might be sponsored three different ways. Also, to facilitate your reading, let's shorten "How To Write Magazine Articles That Sell" to "article writing," "Nurses: How To Write For Publication" to "nurses," and "Proper Memo Writing" to "memos."

Seminar location

Where would participants at an "article writing" seminar expect it to be held? Where would they expect to attend it? Both the feasibility study and common sense will suggest answers.

Your feasibility study will show that similar seminars are held in two places: at academic institutions and at hotels or public meeting places. The first are offered by the extended education departments of colleges and universities. The latter seem to be sponsored directly by the speaker or in conjunction with other speakers, though the fact that the promotion uses a company name reduces that to supposition.

Sometimes writing seminars are also components of writing conferences usually offered by colleges or religious organizations. These are almost always held at the sponsor's site.

The "nurses" seminar might also be held on a campus, according to your feasibility study, but could as well be held at an institution employing nurses, or at a hotel or public meeting place. These seem to be sponsored by academic and health-related institutions, firms specializing in such seminars, and professional nursing oranizations and publications. Many are self-sponsored. Seminars are also included in conferences or conventions for nurses.

Participants at a "memo" seminar would expect to attend it where they work or where they are sent, since the benefactor of their improved skills would primarily be the company they work for. Said in reverse, unless fully paid to do so, employees would not likely attend such a seminar offered elsewhere during off-work hours if the purpose of such attendance was only to make their employer richer!

Pay range

How much one might pay to attend your seminar is important to know because later you must estimate promotional costs, and the approximate potential income must be balanced against those costs to see which form of sponsorship would be the most profitable. It is also important to know if the seminar participant expects to pay the fee by himself or for it to be paid by someone else.

Again, your feasibility study should show you a range of fees commonly charged for seminars similar to your own. Another factor must also be considered: how central to the participant's earning power is the topic of your seminar?

Seminars on writing are a good example. Few expect to survive solely from their writing, at least when they begin. Most write during their free hours, consider it a creative avocation, and are drawn to it, in part, because other than a typewriter the costs are minimal. Writing can bring a steady income, even a huge profit, but for most it will remain an enjoyable outlet of expression.

There's another factor too: most writers figure that they can write with or without your help. After all, they've been doing it since they were kids! And even though you will tell them how to sell what they write as well, which most can't do, that too seems secondary, something they will "get to" or "learn on their own." So they don't see the dire necessity of paying for your information.

On the other hand, if you gave a seminar that showed how to turn kitchen spoons into gold, you could charge a bundle, speak on the top of a mountain at 3 a.m., and a rainstorm wouldn't deter the eager crowds. They would see immediate benefits, knowledge they must get from you, and the possibility of cashing in quick.

So how much they will pay to attend your seminar is directly related to the perceived value they attach to your seminar, how much they need what you say, how many other ways they can get that information, how applicable that information is to solving their need, and how quickly the information can be converted into the benefit -- cash, security, beauty, happiness, whatever -- that is pulling them to the seminar in the first place.

For "article writing" they will expect to pay anywhere from $25-75, with the typical fee about $40. That will include a workbook and a talk that will last from three to eight hours.

The information concerning the nursing seminar is based on California, where nurses are required to earn approved continuing education units for periodic license renewal. It assumes that the "nurse" seminar has been approved by the Board of Registered Nursing. Some seminars are offered at the institutions where the nurses work and, if not free, are nominally priced. Others cost from $30-150, with about $50 for an eight-hour program common.

Participants would not expect to pay for the "memo" seminar since it is for job improvement. If you are to be paid it must be by the firm, which would hire you to offer the program to its employees.

Identification and Contact

Who would be the top priority registrants for each seminar? For "article writing" the most likely registrants would be people at large who want to be in print in nonfiction. For "nurses" the most likely registrants would be, as you can guess, nurses! And for "memos" it would be company employees who must or should write memos.

The question is how would you most effectively identify and contact these top priority registrants.

Writers-to-be among people at large are the hardest to identify. If you ran full-page ads in the newspaper, broadcast lengthy commercials on radio and TV, and sent a flyer to each home you'd surely get the message to most of them. But that's far too expensive; any one of those means alone would cost far more than you could recover. Yet how else do you draw out one segment of the populace other than give the information to all and let those interested step forward? Would-be writers look and act much like other humans. The way to identify them is to advertise the seminar in such an appealing way that those truly interested would identify themselves by registering.

For "nurses" your problem is solved. All you have to do is rent a mailing list of as many nurses registered with the state (or registering unit) as you wish, send them flyers, and stand back. This can be supplemented by contacts with institutions that use nurses, the nursing teaching facilities, and nurses' professional organizations and publications.

The "memo" registrants are even more easily found: they work for the business where you will offer your seminar. Your problem here is identifying firms (or groups of any kind) that have memo writing needs, then convincing them that you should be hired to meet those needs. Once you are hired, your registrants will attend as part of their job. You needn't convince them; you must convince their bosses!

Cost per contact

If it costs you $100 to attract every registrant for your $50 seminar, you'd better find a less expensive means of attraction or get out of seminaring pronto! On the other hand, if you can fill a hall at $5 a head and collect $50 each, you've found your calling.

So here you must ask how -- by what means -- you can make that contact, and of those means which is the least expensive.

Our first example, "writing articles," is the most complicated because it has the most variables. You could advertise it yourself: radio or TV, newspapers, flyers, plus free forms of supplementary promotion. Or you could let another group pay for the promotion in exchange for part of your income.

Let's do some quick figuring here, saving the details about promotion to a later chapter. You noted earlier that participants at public writing seminars would pay from $25-75, with $40 about average. If a good crowd is 25 and you charged that $40 apiece, you would bring in $1000. You also found that most of these seminars were co-sponsored with colleges/universities or were self-sponsored and offered at hotels or public meeting halls.

If you were to self-sponsor this seminar you would have a budget of $1000 potential income. You must rent a hall, so figure $75 for a half-day, leaving $925. It is fairly common to allocate from 50-65% of the anticipated income for promotion, to draw registrants to the door. Say you budget 60% of that $925, or $555. Three questions immediately present themselves:

(1) how many people can you attract through the mass media for $555?

(2) can you pay the rest of the expenses -- your travel and food, workbooks, incidental expenses -- from the remaining $370?

(3) is it worth the time and effort to offer this seminar for what remains of the $370 after expenses?

There is no guarantee that by spending $555 on promotion -- a tiny budget to be scattered over the general populace -- that you will attract anybody, and that the entire amount won't be spent on a seminar that will have to be cancelled. That is, of course, always the risk of self-sponsoring. You could charge the seminar participants $75 a person, raising your promotion budget to $1122. But will twice the promotion sell any more registrations at nearly twice the cost? However one juggles the numbers it looks foolhardy to self-sponsor this seminar until one has a better grasp on harder facts.

The second approach might be to let another group pay the promotion in exchange for part of the income. By good fortune that is precisely what most extended education programs do: they include your program in their schedule for that quarter or semester; provide a room or facility; handle preregistrations; promote your seminar through their catalog, flyers, and press releases, and either pay you a prearranged fee or a percentage of the income. The most appealing element is the inclusion of your seminar write-up in the catalog that may be distributed to anywhere from 50,000 to several hundred thousand homes, depending upon the size of the community and the school's outreach.

Let's say that the college extension program pays 55% (most range from 50-60%). If the charge is $40 and your seminar does attract

25 participants, you earn $550. For that amount you provide workbooks, yourself properly attired, a super seminar, and whatever paperwork (sign-up sheets, evaluations, handouts) required. That's $550 risk-free income, minus travel, food, and accommodations. Best yet, if 50 show up that would be $1100. And if nobody is bright enough to register for your program, all you would lose would be the cost of the workbooks!

Is there any question that in this case **co-sponsorship with an academic institution** makes the most sense?

With the "nurse" seminar our choice will be precisely the reverse. Let's use some actual numbers to show why.

Here you are considering four possible sponsors: academic institutions, self-sponsorship, booking through companies that offer seminars to nurses, or the institutions employing nurses offering in-service training. Rather than considering all four at once, you might set aside the last two until you determine what the schools or self-sponsorship might yield, to see if either would still be appealing.

Using the same figures as above -- an academic institution paying 55% of the registration fees -- for an eight-hour program costing $50, you could earn $687.50.

Yet, using Los Angeles as an example, you might send a flyer by mail to each of the 10,000 nurses in the greater Los Angeles area telling of four identical seminars that you will be offering over a two-week period at four geographically separated spots, each costing the same $50 for eight hours of BRN-approved credit. (The flyer cost might be $2200: 11 cents postage, 7 cents for printing, 3 cents for each address, and a penny for the mailing service.) Other than your flyer expense and incidental mail and phone order costs (say $150), your other expense would be meeting rooms that would hold up to 75 people each for a day, which might run $150 each. So your total expense would be $2950.

There is no magic response rate for flyers -- variables abound -- but a 2% response is fairly reasonable for a well planned, benefit-laden flyer sent to a tightly-identified market like nurses. So if we do draw registrations at that rate, the income will be $ 10,000 -- for a rough profit of $ 7050. (Even a 1% registration response rate would bring a profit of $2050.)

The question here is whether you have the $2950 to gamble, because however well stocked you are with facts self-sponsorship never ceases to be a gamble. Or could you find four academic institutions in that same area that would offer your program, and you might earn $2750, risk-free?

What about companies offering seminars to nurses or an "in-service" program at a hospital? Check them out. If you find a group that will pay you more, that's your answer. That is so unlikely, however, let's set both aside right now.

For the "nurse" seminar, then, if you have the cash and nerves, it's **self-sponsorship**, an extensive mailing, four programs, and a wheelbarrow for the profits.

There has never been much doubt about the "memo" seminar. It would fail as a public program because far too few people would attend on their own to learn what they perceive as a "company skill." Therefore self-sponsoring or co-sponsoring with a college wouldn't make much sense.

Clearly, this is an **"in-house"** program to be given to businesses, the government, or any other large organization where size and policy make memos necessary and important. How much you can earn from this seminar depends on how much it is worth to the sponsors, which in turn will be predicated upon how well you identify groups with a memo-writing need and how well you package and sell your program to them.

We now have determined the most appropriate initial forms of sponsorship for the three examples posed. What remains, then, is actually contacting the desired sponsors, double-checking our facts and assumptions, and, should this choice stand as the most appropriate, getting booked.

Chapter 10

Getting Booked

Booking becomes a problem only when you are offering seminars through others. Three major groups do most of the seminar booking: academic/institutional sponsors, professional or trade associations, and businesses (for in-house, licensed/customized, or public presentations).

Yet that assortment of sponsors works primarily in one of two ways: you approach them or they approach you.

You Approach The Sponsor

For beginners it invariably starts with you making the first approach. Which makes sense since you have the idea, you can meet others' needs, and you have the means -- a seminar. But the sponsor doesn't know that and probably doesn't know you, and surely knows others with similar wares to hawk.

So that is your challenge: to make you and your service worth the risk to sponsor. Let's explain by showing how one typically might book through a university extended education program. (Later we will explain how booking differs for the other sponsors that you must approach.)

Academia:

Utopia University is located at the edge of a large city. Its Extended Education Division offers hundreds of well attended non-credit programs and mails 100,000 bulletins (which those not affiliated call "catalogs") to the homes in that city and the neighboring suburbs. You want to offer a seminar through Utopia U.

First you must read both that bulletin and Utopia's regular course catalog to see which programs and courses come closest to your topic. If that is being taught for credit, you must be accepted on the faculty, or at least be approved by the academic department, before you can offer a similar course through extension. That can take months or years, sits perilously close to the gray area of credit/no-credit conflict, and is simply best avoided by changing your topic or seeking another sponsor.

Assuming there is nothing similar to your seminar, the next step is to call the Extended Education office and explain that since you are interested in proposing a seminar that you would like to offer there, to whom should a letter be addressed and are there other forms to be completed and submitted with that letter? You will be given a name and title to contact. If other forms are needed, ask that they be sent to you.

You might be transferred by phone to the person to whom you should write, so you should have in mind a title and a basic structure for your program, plus an idea of who would benefit from attending. (In most cases it's best to avoid this phone contact since your letter and attachments will make a better first impression.)

Your initial letter, in business form, should gently sell your idea, the seminar, and you as a person to speak about it. Tell why you are qualified to offer that seminar. If it has been given elsewhere, explain when and where, and list the name, position, and address/phone of the person directly responsible for the offering.

Describe those who would likely attend such a seminar, why, and how they could be reached: through the bulletin, sending brochures to a mailing list, ads in professional journals, etc. Indicate when you would like to offer your program -- next quarter, in the spring, etc. -- as well as how many hours it takes and what should be charged each participant. Tell whether a workbook will be included and if you will prepare it; any peculiar room requirements needed (other than a classroom); and any unusual audio-visual needs you will have.

Two pages are plenty. You may wish to append and mention in your letter (1) a current resume that includes your academic background, (2) a description sheet of the seminar as it might appear in the bulletin, (3) the best of your testimonial letters from other extended education directors, sponsors, or even participants, and (4) a seminar outline. Plus, of course, any additional forms Utopia U. sent to be returned with your cover letter.

The result? One of three. No reply. No. Or yes, usually qualified.

If there's no reply in, say, two or three weeks (academic wheels grind very slowly), call the person to whom the letter was addressed and kindly ask about the state of consideration of your proposal. Don't rant or pass out if it hasn't arrived. Academic wheels also grind up letters or throw them away. So always keep a copy of everything, and send a copy of that copy. Be patiently persistent.

If it's a "no," ask why. If there they are offering something similar to it, suggest another seminar that doesn't overlap. If there is doubt about you or the proposal, ask how that doubt can be eliminated.

If it's a "yes," the director will usually want to meet with you to iron out the details. Dress up appropriately, be businesslike, and explore the possibility, if this draws as well as you expect, of expanding later with related seminars in the same field. But gently. It's more important that you nail down a date and location (if possible), and that you understand the payment policy, when payment is made, and anything else you need to know to serve that school professionally.

What's your real opposition? Yourself, if you don't present your ideas in an articulate, professional, confident (but not cocky) manner. And the rest of the speakers. The bulletin has just so many pages, the buildings have just so many rooms, and the staff can handle just so many programs. So you must nudge your way into those limitations. Once in and drawing well, it's easier to expand.

Professional/trade associations:

Your approach differs only a bit here. You must still put something impressive in that booker's hands that shows why you should talk to the members.

Often you are a member of the group, or a member group, of the association you want to address, so you can substitute some of the initial information gathering by speaking directly to the programmer. And since you are a member, you will be closer to knowing precisely what the group wants to hear.

But for the details the rest is the same. You must sell yourself.

Businesses:

The method of approaching business meeting planners for speeches and seminars is nearly identical, and it is well explained in the second half of this book by Mike Frank. So let me focus on a few details as they specifically pertain to seminars (or workshops, as they are more often called here).

The first problem in booking "in-house" presentations is finding the person who does it. They carry a dozen titles. The easiest way is to call the switchboard and explain that you want to mail information to the person who books or contracts workshops at the firm. Would they please give you that person's name, position, and the address of their office?

A letter follows, but in this case a letter no longer than a page, with only those attachments that are absolutely necessary, if any. (More people unsell themselves by over-writing and sending unnecessary information than make a sale.) The letter really asks for an appointment of, say, 10 minutes to explain why that firm would benefit from "---------" workshop. The letter must give the essentials -- your name, what you offer, who benefits and how, references of pleased clients, and the request for an appointment. Indicate that you will call them at a certain hour on a certain date (a week or 10 days after they receive the letter). And call.

The meeting is crucial. In ten minutes you must show how they can benefit from your services and what you do -- longer if they are indeed interested. So you must be prepared, positive, and properly attired. The rest is details about the seminar/workshop itself.

Mind you, everything must have the appearance of success: stationery, clean copy, handsome display workbook, your appearance. The workshop must follow suit.

"Licensed/customized" presentations aren't sold this way. You don't knock on the door. They call you or knock on your door.

But you can sell your seminar-giving skills to other seminar-giving firms. They usually have the format and handout material prepared and expect you to learn a script to their program, so you won't be selling your seminar, just your speaking skills.

Check with others in your field of specialization about seminar-givers, and if you are interested in joining their staff, send a letter that tells about you, how you can help them, and asks for an appointment. At the appointment show what you have done as a speaker, look dynamic and prosperous, dress appropriately, and be articulate. How could they possibly reject a combination like that?

The Sponsor Approaches You

Don't count on it! At least in the beginning you spend much of your time attempting to convince others to take a risk on you, with scant tools to justify that wish!

But at some point someone will ask if you'd like to offer a seminar or workshop to his group or organization. Don't leap up and down and shout about how your ships have all come home! Make an appointment with him to work out the details. Find out if he has the authority to do the booking, and if not suggest that the person who does also be at the meeting.

You cannot afford to be any less professional because the sponsor sought you than you'd be the other way around, and that must be the guiding beacon in the actions that follow.

Your being contacted is most likely to happen when a large firm wants a customized program developed. Often it follows a successful consultation you've had with them. They like what they saw, feel that you could help them in another way, and the phone rings.

But mostly seminar-giving follows sponsor-hunting -- or you giving them on your own. Booking isn't hard when you have the solution to a need well defined and ready to share. Put yourself professionally between the needy and a group that benefits from helping them solve their need and booking is almost irresistible.

Chapter 11

Five–Step Guide
for Seminar Success

We have spoken of some elements vital to success in seminar-giving -- particularly subject selection, description, title, and market identity. We will expand upon that base with other elements no less important to draw participants to the offering.

At this junction, however, a "Five-Step Guide For Seminar Success" might be most properly inserted, as a checklist for those organizing seminars as well as a review for those already practicing the trade.

These steps are specifically applicable to public seminars, since most seminar-givers begin in the public realm. With only slight modification the same steps apply to all seminars, however organized or financed.

(1.) The subject must be appealing and clearly stated in the title and description, plus it must meet a need sufficiently strong that one will pay to attend.

That is, the person must be attracted to the subject by the title, which is reinforced and expanded in the description. He must see the seminar as a way to meet a need. It must be clear why he should attend. The benefits must be stated or obvious: by attending the seminar he will solve personal problems, get rich, learn a skill that will ultimately result in a raise or a more responsible position, find security, overcome frustrations, improve his sex life, ...

This is the single most important guideline of the five. The best promotion, finest location, and most attractive fee imaginable will not sell a senseless title or a garbled, pointless description any more than you would believe a man dressed in tatters, with manure on his shoes and food in his hair, who told you that, for a fee and a few hours of your time, he would show you how to become rich and successful.

(2.) The seminar must be scheduled when and where the public will attend.

Naturally, you say. That's obvious. But how many have tried to offer seminars about personal safety at nighttime -- the very hours when those most worried about their safety won't leave their homes? Or seminars that teach how to make your boss richer, by improving your skills or efficiency, during your nonworking hours?

If you are offering a seminar that shows how to turn marbles instantly into rubies, you can charge a bundle, give it atop a mountain at 3 a.m., and throw in a whip-toothed rainstorm to test the participants' mettle. The throngs would joyously haul their glass spheroids to wherever you are whenever you speak!

But most of us offer programs markedly less glittering. To us the time and place are proportionately more important to our seminar's success.

(3.) The cost must be in line with perceived benefits and other ways of realizing those benefits.

"Perceived" is the key word. The benefits can be there but if one doesn't perceive them -- why they are worth having or that they can be gained from your seminar -- any cost will be too high.

Assuming that the benefits are not only perceived, they are desired, then your seminar must be affordable and in line with other means of getting those benefits. For example, if your seminar costs $100 and one virtually identical costs $35, where do you think the participants will go? On the other hand, if you are explaining a crucial "how-to" link absolutely necessary to securing $10,000+ contracts and yours is the only program fully sharing that information, isn't a fee of $500 or more worth the investment?

Your main competition is other seminars, and sometimes wildcat consultants. Rarely will taped programs have more appeal than a live presentation, and books, though they may cost only a fraction as much, will be a factor only when your seminar is considered marginal by the participants, when your audience is already book-oriented, or when it is highly price-conscious. Very few will opt to attend a class lasting from several to many weeks when they feel that a seminar can cover the core material adequately.

(4.) The participant must know of the seminar's existence and be attracted to it.

If one has an idea that is salable as a seminar, promotion is usually the difference between success or failure. For though it may be the best idea imaginable, a foolproof way to solve the most pressing need, if nobody knows about it who will attend? Without promotion, who will read the title and description and hurry to register before the hall fills?

Yet promotion is also the greatest financial risk. Self-promoted seminars often take as much as two-thirds of their anticipated income to attract registrants before a penny is made. Promotion properly done can draw crowds to seminars that are promotable. But if the topic, title, description, timing, location, and all the rest aren't right, that is, if the seminar isn't promotable, all of the costs spent making your seminar known may be useless -- or at least ultimately profitless.

So here's where the dice are thrown and the gamble is made: promotional means, content, cost, and repetition. All seminars must be promotable. All must be promoted. The rest is risk.

(5.) The seminar's content and your presentation are crucial for long-term success.

If you are going to offer the seminar time and again -- and why would you go to so much trouble if you weren't? -- what you say and how you say it will be its own best long-term promotion.

Neither the actual content nor your presentation will attract participants to your first seminar. They will register by what you tell them you will say: by the title, description, and the promotional promises. Like a book, first-timers buy seminars by the cover. They don't know if you're a bumbler or have a tongue of honey. They buy on faith.

But if you don't come through, your future is tainted, for nothing is more forceful or harder to erase than negative word-of-mouth.

Therefore, the first time out you must provide not only solid content and professional presentation, particular attention must be paid to the first four steps of this guide so that the number of bearers of positive word-of-mouth is large. Over time the content and presentation, if good, will reduce the risk of promotion and will provide the desired cushion of profit, as long as the first three steps in this guide are properly tended to.

In the business realm, content and presentation are particularly critical from the outset. The first question a potential programmer will ask is "Where did you give this seminar before?" Those references will then be asked, "Is he any good?" And you will be booked primarily from the responses of those who heard you perform. Businesses don't take the risks that the public must. Thus the first business booking is extremely hard to get. Later bookings are far easier when that reply is, "He's super. The best money you'll ever spend." That's why content and presentation, properly done, are money in the bank.

SECTION TWO

"THOSE PESKY DETAILS"

Chapter 12

Organization and Content

Since seminars are offered in topics as diverse as stuffing sausages and unstuffing fatties, it's impossible to devise a master scheme that works equally well for the organization and content of every program.

Yet there is a technique that sits at the heart of most successful seminars, workshops, books, articles, and other forms of idea dissemination.

We spoke of a working question. From the working question comes first the organization, then the content. Here's how it works.

Your seminar is called "How To Train for the Triathlon," so the working question is "How does one train for the triathlon?" You simply take the title and put it in question form. (If your title doesn't lend itself to that, look again at that title. It's likely to mislead those registering for your seminar.)

From the working question, then, ask the secondary questions that naturally flow. Such as:

(1.) What is a triathlon? What sports and distances are involved, and in what order are the sports performed?

(2.) Who would and could train for one? Men and women? Beginning and ending at what ages? How would the training differ by age?

(3.) How far in advance would one begin training? What goals are the trainees pursuing: to finish, a set time, an "ideal" time calculated by age and sex?

(4.) Where would one train? Would it matter if he/she lived in different climatic areas at different times of the year? Would cost be a factor in the training? Diet, attire, mental state?

(5.) What physical and emotional condition must the person be in to train for a triathlon? Are there pre-training steps to be taken to reach the necessary condition?

Plus a dozen more questions one could draw from the working question.

You then take all of these secondary questions and put them in logical order so that their answers, collectively and sensibly, respond to the working question.

For example, some working questions require a chronological response. If, in a pickle, you decide to offer a seminar called "How to Grow Cucumbers," you might start from what you do first and work to the final action, from buying the seed and breaking the soil to the final harvesting. A seminar built around such a working question would be organized in that way, chronologically.

Others are organized developmentally. Our triathlon example would be best presented that way, though chronology also enters in. You start with an undertrained person and explain the goals. You determine a reasonable time to complete your first competition in swimming, cycling, and running, plus the equipment needed in each for prime performance. A diet and training regimen is established, and so on.... It's similar to building a wall from the bottom brick up.

Still others organize seminars around opposite models, most often a "winner" and "loser." Or they take a complex set of actions, isolate a specific set of variables, and show how one set of skills and actions will lead to a different and successful result.

The organization is how you answer your working question in the most intelligible way. It's how you build that wall bottom up into the unique form you have chosen. The content is the type and variety of bricks needed to do the job.

For our triathlon seminar we may decide to focus on four things: goals, time, mental preparation, and physical preparation, and answer the other questions through these subdivisions.

The four-part structure and the developmental approach are the organization. The material used to explain and illustrate that structure is the content. How one defines the goals, how those goals differ by sport and age-sex of the participant, when they are to be attained, the ways that the physical and psychological goals differ and where they overlap, examples of others' goals and means of realizing them, and so on -- those might be the contents of the first part of that organization.

Why would one build the organization and contents from a working question? Because by doing so it's virtually impossible not to work from the core of the topic. Which is the most common complaint by seminar-takers of other programs not so designed: the speakers don't say anything about the subject!

The quality of the answers to those questions, that is, the choice of the contents used to explain and illustrate, is the difference between a passable and an exceptional seminar. Two things particularly enhance that quality: research and clarity of thought and expression.

The content of many seminars comes from the speaker's personal experience. Yet few experiences are so comprehensive, despite the years over which they might spread, that research can't add depth, breadth, and sharper perspective. That can be farther extended by including an annotated bibliography in the workbook, to fit the personal experience into the broader readings in the field.

To clarify the thought and expression of your seminar, explain terms not commonly used, simplify to make your points, and use examples and quotations to vary your presentation. Then if your seminar still isn't understood by everyone there, clarify more.

Winston Churchill may well have had seminars in mind when he said, "Old words are better than new, short words are better than long." Why purposely obfuscate when "to make unclear" says it so much simpler for so many more people?

A final tool of clarity can be audio-visual aids. Seeing is often far easier to comprehend than hearing. Overhead (opaque) projections, slides, and flip charts are usually the easiest a-v tools to integrate into a presentation. Whatever form is used, it must add enough in content and clarity to offset the time required for its set-up, display, and dismantling. (To reduce the set-up and tear down time, arrange for the visuals to be shown before or after a break.)

There is no single, magic form of organization that always works for every program. The working question, the secondary questions, and the contents used to answer them, will determine the way your seminar is structured and presented. The result, however, must be a program that does what its title promises, is interesting and clearly understood, and leaves its listeners not only fully informed but eager to attend another seminar you offer.

Chapter 13

Timing: Length, Dates, Days, Hours

There are really three questions related to time or timing:

(1.) How long should the seminar last?
(2.) What dates or days are best for seminars?
(3.) What hours on those days are best?

LENGTH

"How long should the seminar last?" Abraham Lincoln, when asked how tall a man should be, said just tall enough for his feet to touch the ground.

A seminar should be just long enough to do what it intends. If it proposes to explain how to use a new computer software program and can do so fully and clearly in one three-hour session, that seminar should last three hours. Any less and the purpose can't be realized; any longer and you needlessly waste the valuable time of your participants.

That answer is little help, though, when attempting to put a time limit on a new seminar. The starting question in that case is "how do you determine the right length for a new seminar?" A continuing question for all seminars is when do you ever know when it has done what it proposes "fully and clearly" for all in attendance?

The latter answer comes from responses to evaluations, questions asked by participants after the sessions have ended, the look in their eyes as the seminar is being given, and the results of any seminar-ending test (should that be part of your structure). Time adjustments, once a seminar has been offered successfully over a stretch of time, are progressively less likely. More often an occasional purge of extraneous illustrative material is required to keep the presentation lean and the intent realized within the previously satisfactory time range.

How do you determine the right length for a new seminar?

We have already discussed the "working question." To make an educated guess at an ideal length for the seminar you must know what must be said, explained, demonstrated, and collectively done at the session to "fully and clearly" answer the "working question," plus all pertinent secondary questions that flow from it, then calculate approximately how long each of those activities and responses will take.

Add to that the length of time needed for questions from the participants and satisfactory answers from you. Remember that you need a comfortably paced introduction or opening plus a conclusion that will reinforce or at least restate what was learned. Finally, your audience will commend you to heaven for having a sufficient number of breaks properly spaced!

Finally, you must finish on time. Nothing is less appreciated than a professional speaker who drones on after the appointed hour. Participants put their faith in you to deliver the message within a stated time. Exceed that final hour and everything you have done up to then can be negatively tainted.

From these guesstimates you can determine a rough length of time needed for your presentation. Check that against the scheduled time of on-going seminars about the same or similar topics. What are you going to offer that those presenters don't? What will you delete? Will that account for the difference in time?

In addition to the length of other seminars there are some logical reasons that will help you frame your program's time perimeters -- or will help you rethink the breadth of your working question.

Is there an ideal length for a seminar?

There are preferred time lengths and reasons why programs aren't too short or too long, but "ideal lengths," if they exist at all, vary according to the kinds of seminars given and the expectations and sitting endurance of the participants.

For **seminars that the general public must pay to attend,** 3.5 to 4 hours seem to be the most sought lengths. Less than that, particularly anything under three hours, and people often have trouble justifying getting dressed up, finding a sitter for the kids, driving to the site, parking the car, finding the room, and taking the notes for such a modest information return. Longer than four or 4.5 hours seems eternal to those no longer attuned to learning by sitting. The death knoll seems to be when a seminar must be scheduled around lunch or supper since that adds another 60-90 minutes to the total time.

One must remember that school -- the sitting and learning part -- evokes negative memories in many people, thus a seminar with a similar format will be rejected outright by some who say "I can't (read 'won't') sit for that long!" Even the term "seminar" sounds academic. So if you are planning a seminar for folks who predominantly fall in this category, you might call your program a "workshop," keep the length short (3.5 to 4 hours), and emphasize the hands-on elements of the program. That is sometimes best done by including an actual activities schedule in your description, with two breaks clearly indicated.

For **seminars that professionals will attend,** the time length is far more elastic. Professionals know that good things come from sitting and listening, like degrees, certificates, licenses, and the later freedom that increased income and gathered knowledge can bring. Furthermore, they have trained themselves to sit for longer periods of time!

Some professional seminars will last for days, and one-day programs are common. The longer the program, however, the greater the need to bring in more speakers and to vary the modes of presentation, with a-v support, small group sessions, etc.

Many professional seminars will be offered for academic credit or c.e.u.'s (continuing education units). The credit-granting or authorizing body will state the number of hours of attendance required to receive the credit, so that will dictate the length of your seminar. If credit isn't given it is usually wise to offer some form of participation recognition for your longer programs. Attractive certificates can be printed locally at a modest cost. Whether you give credit or award certificates upon completion should be prominently mentioned in the promotion. Such "extras" have a powerful drawing power.

For the **first of a two-part seminar,** usually a short "teaser" to explain the benefits and attract the participant to the follow-up element(s), a session from 1-3 hours is common. Since it is free, generally located in an easily accessible place, and given at a time when it is particularly convenient, people will attend to see what the program is all about.

The length of time for an **in-house program** will be worked out between you and the firm or group. Two major considerations come into play here. Every minute the employee is at your program, plus the time spent getting there and back to his desk or station, is lost productivity to the firm. And many companies have rigid eating hours that they would rather not change. So in-house program-givers must be particularly time-conscious. And most programs, if given at the site, must be completed in the morning or afternoon to be worked around that lunch schedule.

What about breaks?

Everybody loves a seminar break! Your listeners need to exercise their legs and get their systems in motion. Your voice needs rest. Washrooms beckon. Thirst is abated. People become acquainted or renew friendships.

You just can't have too few or too many, and there's the rub. A rule of thumb used by many speakers calls for two breaks in four hours, with the first about an hour into the talk and the second somewhere in the middle of the time remaining. The first break is often 15 minutes long, the second 10-15.

Unless there is a reason not to do so, it makes sense to tell the listeners the number of breaks and approximate timing of each during the introduction. Then before the first break indicate the location of the washrooms, food, and other items of particular interest. Give them the precise time you expect them back. If you too are planning a washroom respite, edge toward the door as you offer the advice to the others, then sprint like a spirit!

A final thought. On the rarest of occasions something disruptive will occur. It might be a jackhammer on the floor above, a bellicose drunk suddenly out of control, or another seminar-giver claiming (with a crowd to his rear) that the room is his. That is the time for a 10-minute break to solve the problem. (And somewhat shorter breaks later to pick up lost time -- or creative pruning of the contents to leave in the essentials but still not run overtime.)

DATES

The best dates are very much related to the subject and the participants. April is a terrible time for seminars for tax consultants; mid-winter is as poor for ski instructors. The real question is when are the people most likely to attend?

I've found that June is poor for teacher-directed seminars. They are worn out in June, go on vacation then or in July, but are getting antsy to return to the classroom in August and early September. So late August is a very good time to appeal to teachers with a seminar program.

Yet if the legislature passes a law obliging every teacher to attend, say, a three-hour session about computers and the classroom, sets the deadline at one year, and will lift the teacher's certification if the requirement is not fulfilled, virtually any weekend or evening (save holidays) will draw well. It gets back to motivation or push.

Thus if a topic is "hot," get scheduling. In this category are new laws or tax interpretations touching business or large organizations.

New ways for the public to make or save money, fads that cut close to the pocketbook or personal vanity, trends in style or color or exercise, new means of diet or habit control -- strike while the newness draws.

Regarding specific dates, avoid conflicts with major events in the same city that will either attract your potential audience or will tie up traffic and parking. Occasionally TV or political events will detract from your draw: a seminar for show folk shouldn't be scheduled on the evening of the Academy Awards.

Avoid booking on three-day holidays. Families use those to go elsewhere or do things as a unit. The entire weekends are disrupted, and even the evening before and the day after are negatively influenced where your seminar is concerned.

Climatic conditions can't be ignored. While those living where snow abounds in the winter grow used to overcoming the obstacle, there are days -- and particularly nights -- when people simply can't leave home. Air conditioning helps offset the worst ravages of summer, but for many the coming and going are too unpleasant to brave.

If you are speaking to paycheck cliffhangers you'd best schedule after payday. The military and public employees are good examples, since they are usually paid monthly. Anybody booking the week before had better have a super program **and** offer credit card registration. The rest should wait a week.

Last, whole regions have times when seminars must, by necessity, be missed. If your audience consists mostly of farmers, planting and harvesting will keep it from your doors. Tourists tie up the locals at favored sites with seasonal jobs. College towns empty out on holidays and most of the summer.

You're saying, "of course, all of that's obvious." Yet there's not a seminar-giver active who hasn't overlooked the obvious. And when you deal with specific clientele, like the C.P.A.'s at tax time and the skiers during winter, you must determine what is obvious, what is peculiar to your participants, and when they are eagerly hunting for the very thing you want to sell.

My own experience booking through schools? Best months, in order: April, March, July, October, late September. Worst months? December (after about Dec. 5), later May, June, and January. Few exceptions on the strong side; delightful surprises in the weaker periods.

DAYS

Again from my experience mainly at the college/university level through extended education, and my friends', mostly with public and corporate programs: once you find out the best periods or dates you can deduce the best days.

At the college/university level, Monday (day or evening) is the worst weekday, Tuesday through Thursday are strong and about the same, Friday is weaker but a short and not too involved evening program can draw well, Saturday afternoon is just a bit better than the morning (if your audience includes some who must work until noon) but the evening is fatal, and Sunday afternoon draws well for husband/wife or family programs. Sunday evening, oddly, will draw but the seminar should end by about 9 p.m.

Whether you schedule during the week (day or night) or on the weekend is determined by who benefits from the participation. If the primary benefactor is the company for which the participant works, that is, if the person is going to improve skills or knowledge to perform a job better, then it should be scheduled during working hours so the person will be released and paid to attend. But if the participation is avocational, for the person's own betterment or growth, then it should be booked at night or on the weekend.

If you are scheduling with a company, your seminar or training session will be booked during the firm's regular working hours. The exception will be when they want you to offer a lunchtime program or to take part in a retreat, often at a distant location, sometimes over a weekend or holiday.

HOURS?

The best hours will be determined by you and the firm where your program is offered on a closed basis. Presumably the times selected will be those best for the firm and the participants.

But when you schedule public seminars, night hours fall between 6 and 10 p.m. Only when you deal with school teachers, who can attend on-site programs earlier, does it make sense to think of booking before people can grab a quick supper and drive to the seminar location. Even 6 p.m. is difficult in larger cities with slow-moving traffic. But 10 is non-negotiable. If you list a final hour after 10 you lose huge numbers of potential participants because they will get home too late to be effective the next morning. (Remember, Sunday programs can start earlier but must end by 9 p.m.)

Weekday hours should take into consideration two key factors: when do the participants expect it to begin and how many must arrange for babysitting before they can arrive? If your seminar is for nurses or secretaries, say, who are accustomed to being at work by 8 a.m., you can begin at that same hour -- or at 8:30 if the driving distance is great. But if your audience is housewives in the 20-30 age range, 9 a.m.

or even later will give them time to leave their wards elsewhere before you start. Morning is generally better than the afternoon for public weekday seminars.

Senior citizen programs require more investigation before scheduling. In cities the seniors are often more closely tied to public transit, so seminar scheduling must be integrated with the bus, subway, or elevated schedules. Few seniors like to travel at night, so book them during daylight hours. And often a program from mid-morning, including lunch, and finishing in mid-afternoon will have special appeal. Finally, this group is particularly price-sensitive.

While your weekday hours will generally be 8-12 or 1-5, or segments of those blocks, your Saturday times will likely be 12:30-4:30 or 1-5, with a secondary time of 9-1. Sunday must give participants time to go to church and have lunch, so 1 p.m. is about the earliest starting time, with 5 p.m. about as late as you can go without interrupting Sunday supper.

A final thought about days and hours: in public programming it is far easier to attract an audience to a one-time seminar than to a program that meets more than once. In other words, given a choice of a five-hour weeknight program that must meet in two 2.5-hour sessions or one four-hour program meeting one night, the latter will outdraw the former every time.

But let's say you have six hours you **must** include and it has to be offered on week nights. Then break it into two sessions, 6:30-9:30 each, and offer it either on a Tuesday-Thursday sequence in the same week (or Monday-Wednesday, but that is weaker) or offer it on two consecutive Tuesdays (or Wednesdays or Thursdays). But don't schedule it for two nights in a row.

Chapter 14

Price

By price we mean how much you will charge a person to attend your seminar. In contractual relationships that is not a concern, since the sponsor pays a fee that is only secondarily related to the number of potential participants. In this section, then, let's focus on public and occasionally private seminars and how much you should charge.

A critical question must precede our consideration of how much to charge, however. How important is the income from the registrations? If it is the major income source, the price should be as high as the market will bear and your conscience will abide. What it will bear will be determined by the greatest number of registrants at the most favored fee. If 50 will attend at $50 each, 40 at $75, 38 at $100, and 16 at $125, the $100 rate is the most profitable.

But if the registration fee is secondary and your primary purpose is to attract consulting clients, sell products, or gain exposure for later speaking engagements, then your fee will be altered to match that secondary purpose.

If your major income will be derived from follow-up consulting, you may want to set your registration fee just high enough to pay the meeting and promotion costs, or less, counting on the profit sacrifice and lower charge to attract a larger crowd to be mesmerized by your brilliance, grasp of the field, and obvious ability to solve any problem brought your way. Or you may raise the rate to a sensible point where every person you address qualifies as someone willing to pay well for the information that is at the core of your expertise. Those would also be the people most likely to seek more good information later from an informed, articulate source (like you) -- and be willing to pay the higher consulting fees.

If seminars are a means to gather a crowd to whom you can sell products -- tapes, books, more seminars, swimming pools, a weekend at a resort to buy property or a week at a retreat to learn the dogma -- you must determine first whether any of the basic income must be derived from registrations or whether enough profit will result from later sales to be able to offer the opening seminar free.

We mentioned one-part and two-part seminars earlier. If much but not all of your income will come from back-of-the-room sales, like tapes and books, you will likely offer a one-part seminar, charge a fee low enough to attract large numbers but high enough to help offset the costs.

Yet when the product mark-up is substantial or people simply will not pay to attend if there is a charge, you probably will want to offer two-part seminars, with the first part, usually the "teaser," free. At that presentation you will focus on the need, explain the solution (which you, of course, have for sale), and then convince the listeners to sign up and make a down payment (or, better yet, a full payment) for your product or services.

If the overwhelming purpose is exposure for follow-up speaking, seminars may be a slow road to that destination because seminar participation takes time and the people you wish to impress will likely not have the time to attend just to hear you speak. You might more profitably read the other half of this book, about speaking, where a short talk superbly done, if properly positioned, can quickly yield later speaking commitments. On the other hand, such exposure through any seminar is inevitable. Seminars are excellent examples of how one performs in an extended situation and are good indications of speaking prowess at shorter lengths. But that should be a spinoff purpose, at best.

When the registration fee pays the freight, and anything else is gladly accepted but secondarily anticipated, setting the right fee is important. Too high and you'll face empty rooms and empty coffers; too low and you'll be speaking 360 days a year just to survive. A good first step to setting a fee is to see what the competition is charging.

Find out about other seminars in your field, and related fields, and attend as many as you can as part of your "feasibility study." What did they charge? What was your reaction to that fee? Too high or too low? Would you have paid more? Or was it overpriced? Why? How could you change the seminar to make it worth the fee you paid -- or more? Would raising or lowering the fee have attracted more registrants?

Those are the kinds of questions you should ask about established fees -- before establishing your own. Yet, if the price seemed about right and the person has been offering that seminar successfully over a period of time, you might consider charging the same fee and looking at other variables to attract more people, particularly if you are in direct competition with the other seminar.

After all, if the seminar has been drawing well over time the charge is likely high enough to bring a profit to the giver but low enough to attract an audience. And once you have a starting price to test, you can increase or even decrease it later, as experience suggests.

Let's say that the competition charges $50 for a four-hour program. You might stay at that $50 plateau at the outset and see if other things won't bring a larger crowd your way.

Consider offering your seminar at a different **time slot.** If it's being given on Saturday morning, why not Saturday afternoon? Or Tuesday evening? Or if it is the kind of seminar that both husband and wife would benefit from attending, Sunday afternoon might attract both.

Four hours is a good **time length** for seminars, but could you offer as good a program in 3 1/2 hours? That's an even better length, and competes favorably with your competition because most people value their time more than the cost, if the latter is reasonable. Offering a program longer than four hours is usually heading the wrong direction to attract more participants.

A better **location** might attract more people, particularly if your competition is foolish enough to meet in the middle of a high crime area or at a deserted, empty mansion at midnight. Sometimes the topic and the locale are mismatched: "How To Wear Diamonds and Furs" held in a dingy basement or "The Handyman's Guide to Plumbing" in the Hilton Executive Suite. Try to match the place and the topic.

The **handout material** can directly influence your attendance. Make sure that your promotion indicates what you will give the participants to take home. If the competition mentions nothing, all the more reason to mention take-home material. Go them one better. If they speak of handouts, mention a workbook. If they say workbook, say booklet. But beware of mentioning a book unless the material is more than 24 pages, by postal definition, or 50 pages, according to the Library of Congress. If a book is included, naturally that will be given prominence in the promotion.

There is more than just mentioning the handout material, though. Make it sound valuable, which, as we say in the "workbook" section, it indeed is. Tell why the person would want to attend to receive both the seminar and the handouts. "Workbook worth the price of the seminar itself will be given free to every participant!" You get the idea. Then make sure it is packed full of valuable information.

The most important way to win the price/participation battle, though, is through **promotion.** That's how you win the war of words, though it costs money to promote effectively and the tools at your disposal will, in turn, be limited by the price you must charge to attract a crowd.

There is one other factor you must consider in setting your fee: what's it worth to you.

At some point in determining a seminar price you must ask what you want to make from the presentation. Since a four-hour program really takes about eight hours, by the time you travel, set up, speak, tear down, and return, you might set your value at so much a day. Or so many dollars an hour. You do this to get a sense of whether one or many seminars are worth the doing.

Yet making that determination is easier said than done. Do you count all of the preparation time -- going to other seminars, the workbook, the promotion, writing a description, and so on? Is it figured for one seminar, two, six, or as many as might result? And what do you use as a base line for worth?

Which brings you back to the "whys" of giving seminars in the first place. One might ask if, in the long run, giving seminars is a means to living a more satisfying, better paying life than at present. If so, and assuming that satisfaction is coming from the seminars, your present income can be one gauge. If seminars, once established and a clientele and equitable price are found, will be sufficiently more profitable than your present earnings, or other earnings from other activities, that might be an important indication of whether they are in fact worth doing.

If the answer is no, then either you must seek another path than seminars or you must find another topic or another amalgam of marketing tools to elevate the worth of your offerings to the point of acceptable profitability in which the seminar price is but one of those elements.

Chapter 15

Location

Where you offer the seminar depends upon how it is sponsored, why it is given, and what the participants expect.

It's perfectly imaginable that you could offer a seminar in a swamp -- if the purpose was to study ecology and that was the particular locale under consideration. Many are offered during ocean cruises, either to prepare the floaters for the sights to come or to provide a taxable (or just recreational) purpose for the voyage.

But most seminars are held at companies, on campuses, or in hotels/motels. Such booking sites share the grace of being there, convenient, affordable, comfortable, and in some way expected.

We needn't belabor the location of business seminars held at the business or a location it selects: they are paying the bill and that's their choice. Which is not to say you can't suggest a different setting if there's a solid reason for it, but in the end they will select and you will offer it there -- or not.

The real issue comes when you must choose the location.

How do you select the right location?

The kind of seminar will limit your choices, but the length of the program, the geographic origins of your participants, and the contents of their wallets will also each heavily influence the final choice.

The swamp example shows how the subject could limit your locale. We could conjure up more examples to show other extremes. But one seldom must experience the subject or go to it to discuss it. Programs about selling jets in Borneo, the state of the art concerning Chagas disease, or new geothermal energy tapping techniques can all be explained, without loss of quality, in a room in Sleeper, Missouri.

But don't offer a four-day program in Sleeper! Offer a long program at a setting with either resort amenities or side attractions of particular interest to the participants. If Sleeper were located in Central America and the seminar was about Latin American Studies, that would be far better! In other words, the length of the program will shift the emphasis from the topic to the locale. One asks little more than comfort, security, parking, and central location for a half-day seminar. But the longer the program, the greater the demands on the setting and what else it can provide to make the non-seminar hours enjoyable or conducive to the purpose of the visit.

That, in turn, is influenced by the geographic origins of the participants and how much they will pay for the seminar.

If your participants will be coming from all corners of America you might consider either a central location, like Chicago, or two complete sessions, one in the East and one in the West. The site should be easily accessible to airport linkage and scheduled with sensitivity to early-morning arrivals. Presumably those flying long distances are able to pay the costs of a many-day program. So they will not be satisfied by meeting in a recreation hall or third-class motel meeting/game room.

How do you serve the local participants?

The answer depends upon the classification of participant. In both cases you must select a location in keeping with the cost of the program.

If you are giving a seminar to doctors or company executives, the setting must be sufficiently posh to match their expectations. You can also charge more to afford the softer chairs, better decor, and the look of prosperity. (Mind you, in no case should the locale change the quality of the seminar. Wherever it is held or whatever the cost, your seminar must be the very best you can offer.)

If yours is a mass market seminar you are limited by certain realities: rarely will a person travel more than 100 miles or spend the night for such a program. Thus your offering will be part-day or full-day at most. Virtually every minute at the location, other than breaks, will be spent in session. So the scope of acceptable sites is far broader.

Where you would expect to offer a local program to highly-paid professionals in a hotel/motel conference room or a conference center, this can be expanded for mass market seminars to include college/university classrooms, schools, lodge and similar meeting halls, theaters, park district rooms, banks, churches, libraries, and like locations. Lists of locally available locations are generally available from the Chamber of Commerce, the "yellow pages," a Visitors' Bureau, or by contacting the respective organizations directly.

What is the minimum that seminar participants expect? That the location be decent, secure, easy to find, and conducive to their receiving their money's worth at the program. If notetaking is advised, a writing surface is necessary. They expect nearby parking space that is safe for their cars and themselves and, if they must find lunch or supper during a seminar break, they will expect reasonably-priced restaurants nearby.

Must you provide food?

No. In fact, many seminar-givers urge that lunches or dinners **not** be included as part of the seminar.

One, eating elsewhere offers the participants a chance to meet each other informally outside of the meeting room. (Before dismissing the group to find its food, however, it's best to mention the names of some good nearby restaurants at different price ranges, plus suggest that they may wish to join in small groups both to become better acquainted and because some are less familiar with the local streets.)

The second reason has to do with the food at hotels/motels or similar settings. When it is mass-produced and second-rate, as it usually is, you suffer for it. Then there are always the vegetarians, non-salt eaters, rare meat devotees, and so on who make the ordering akin to planning a military battle.

And it raises the cost considerably. Even providing coffee and rolls in the morning is very expensive, though sometimes necessary and absorbed less conspicuously in the fee. At break time at a mass market seminar you can simply direct the participants to the vending machines.

On the other hand, there are those who make meals (usually lunch) the pivotal element of a seminar. They begin a bit later in the morning, end before rush hour, and invite a top-flight guest speaker to address the gathering over lunch, often with a 30-minute "walking off" break after the repast. The presence of the speaker (included in the promotion) helps draw a larger seminar registration as long as the person and the topic are central to the participants' interest.

Another advantage of including a meal is a reduction or elimination of the seminar room rental, in a trade-off worked with the facilities manager. Thus at times the meal cost will be somewhat absorbed in the room savings.

What about a bar?

Not for a part- or one-day program. The truly devoted can imbibe during the breaks and at lunch (or supper) if they wish, either where they eat or by buying their potations in the bar and bringing them to the meal you serve. But the general reaction against drinking during the seminar will keep it to a minimum unless you urge it.

(Need I say that you should never drink alcohol during your own seminar! If you do sip to keep your throat moist make sure it is clearly marked or known to be a Pepsi, coffee, or something non-intoxicating. Otherwise your presentation may suffer; your participants' perception of it definitely will.)

If you are giving a seminar lasting longer than a day you may wish to offer a cocktail party or a no-host bar at some point during the session. This is often done the evening before a seminar that starts the next morning. Sometimes it precedes a dinner on the first evening of the program; rarely, at the conclusion. (If this is done at the seminar site it can be used as another trade-off with the facilities manager to reduce room and food fees.)

But having alcohol directly available and encouraged at the actual seminar sessions is risky business. Unless, of course, the seminar is about wine-tasting.

Is there any advantage to offering seminars at resorts?

Sure. The participants can write off the trip for tax purposes. Companies may send employees there as a bonus or special reward. The atmosphere will be more casual and perhaps more conducive to freer, more open discussions. And promoting the location as well as the subject will attract more participants than just the subject alone.

But there are as many problems. You must book months or years in advance. You will tie up more money farther in advance. You are limited to participants who can afford expensive trips, and thus to subjects that warrant such costs. Your promotion costs will be far higher. And a weather front or a strike can undo in a week all of the preplanning you've been financing for a year.

With a part-day seminar you can lose the buttons off your shirt -- or win a dozen new shirts. Multiply that a hundredfold for the resort seminar. You lose the whole shirt (and the closet) or you win a brand new wardrobe (and a place in which to wear it).

What are the details I should know about booking at hotels?

Rather than duplicate what is done more fully, let me direct you to Sheila Murray's **How To Organize and Manage a Seminar**, 1983, Prentice-Hall. Her text is mainly directed at public seminars held in hotels, motels, and convention centers. It is full of how-to information, and is particularly good on room set-up, seminar site selection, and facility requirements.

What must I know about using college/university settings?

You will usually meet in a classroom. Since it will generally be at night or on the weekend, the room will be probably be dirty.

That means you must arrive an hour in advance (even 90 minutes before if the group will be over 75). If the door will be locked make certain that the extended education office has requested that it be opened by the campus police prior to that time. (If it is still locked when you arrive, call the extended education office, if it is open, or the police, if it's not.)

First you must pick up the papers and pop cans. Swap the ashcan with one from a nearby room, or dump yours in another so you have a clean receptacle. Then count the chairs. Have a third more than you expect from pre-registration, plus know which nearby room will be empty if your late registration tally is high.

Do you need more chairs, a lectern, a table, an eraser, chalk? The beauty of arriving early is that you can pluck with impunity the needed items from nearby rooms. Do it quickly and early, though, before classes show up for those rooms!

Set up your chairs so you are the focal point. If there are desks and you like to roam while you speak, leave a center and side aisles. If there are tables, it is best to place the chairs so every person looks directly at you. (Never have a chair with its back to you.)

Clean the chalkboards to your rear, as well as all extraneous material from the boards on the side walls. Write the title of your seminar, your name, and any other registration information or numbers the school requires. Add a greeting to that: "Welcome!" or "Glad You Are Here!" or something else pleasant. Somewhere to the side but in direct view list the other seminars you are giving at that school that season: date, day, title, location, hour.

Put a sign on the front door and (if it is braced open to let the participants enter) also at the side of that door with the title of the seminar. When there are two doors, put a sign on that farthest from you asking them to come to the other door to register and receive a workbook. Place a desk in front of the distant door, inside and out, to discourage its use. If the room location is particularly hard to find (colleges have hundreds of such places!) you might place signs along the route with arrows. (This requires you to bring signs, tape, and marking pens.)

No later than 30 minutes prior to the seminar you should have switched into your speaking clothes, found both washrooms, and asked others where the closest food and vending machines are (so you can direct the participants before the first break).

Then it's time to spread out your product display, usually called a "back-of-the-room" table but more likely to be "front-of-the-room" if you are working alone. That completed, lay out your seminar script or reminder sheet, get the registration sheets in order, and unpack your workbooks.

Usually you will want to insert the school's (or your own) evaluation sheet, a follow-up mail order product sheet catalog, and other material into the workbook. This is the time. It must be done before the main thrust of participants arrive. (Invariably some eager souls arrive 45 minutes ahead of time. Let them stay in the room so long as they don't interrupt your activity. You can even get them to help you collate workbooks if you get in a time pinch.)

You must be ready to go 20 minutes before the hour, to greet your group and to check their names off the registration list or to show them the process for late registration. If the group is 50 or more, you can "hire" one of the early arrivals to handle the registration at the door, paying with a copy of one of your books. (You can do the same to handle the product sales after the session.)

From then on it's all show. Make the best of the room by keeping the center of attention on a super seminar. Make the setting so secondary that the listeners "would have sat on stone to hear it."

And since most seminar-givers learn their trade in just such settings, find out what in that setting most disturbs and distracts the participants so that later, before offering programs, you can make the necessary changes.

Should you use your own A-V equipments?

If the programs are local, use your own. Schools reluctantly let extended education use their microphones, projectors, and whatnot. And when they are available they come far too frequently without extension cords, bulbs, or amplification.

It's not much different for hotels, frankly, but when travelling you may not wish to carry the accessories. In that case you should test every piece of equipment a day or at least several hours before the presentation.

At schools the equipment should be loaned free of charge -- when available. At hotels you can expect a podium, movie screen, extension cord, and a listing on the activities board in the lobby at no charge. Beyond that it is negotiable. Make certain that you request everything needed at contract time, that you double-check it all as far in advance as possible, and that it is returned when you leave. If anything doesn't work make that known to the manager so you aren't billed -- or a refund is made.

Chapter 16

Workbooks

Are workbooks necessary if you offer seminars? And must you provide them?

Something is necessary, though full workbooks -- many pages, a full packet of materials -- may not be, depending on the purpose and sponsor of the program. Participants expect to receive something and to have something in hand when they leave, akin to a theater program, a baseball scorecard, or the syllabus to a class. If for no other reason, it is a memento that proves the event took place and they were involved.

Since something is expected, you might as well make it both sensible and of continuing value to yourself. Remember that soon after the seminar is over the person will have forgotten almost all of what you said and even more about you. What will remain will be the hand-out. So that should include on the front page the title of the seminar, your name, any logo or artwork you use, all copyright information, a company name if you use one, an address where you can be reached, and a phone number.

A word about the copyright notation. If you expect to use the material later in an article or book, or simply want to protect the words in that form, you may wish to register the copyright with the Copyright Division of the Library of Congress. (For further details, contact that office at Washington, D.C. 20559. Your congressperson can also send you an information packet with the TX forms included.) Or you may wish simply to use the symbol -- Copyright © 198_ by (your name), filling in the proper year and name -- as well as a statement that will scare off 90% of the potential thieves. (See the symbol and statement used in the front of this book. Use the phrase, "All rights reserved. No part...," in its entirety if you wish. It's not copyrighted!)

What you include in your workbook depends on the form of presentation and how much you want the participant to have available later for direct use.

If your seminar is a hands-on program for civics teachers where you take the morning newspaper, cut it up, and see how many projects can be gleaned from a daily reading, your workbook would likely summarize the process and contain a few pages about other ways the exercise might be applied.

But if it is how to set up and market seminars, and the program is packed with facts and how-to material, the participants will need a much fuller workbook. They will be swamped with information anyway, and few will be able to take full notes and retain enthusiasm for many hours.

In either case, though, your workbook should never be a transcription of the seminar itself. Or why would they pay $40-400 to attend, just to receive a packet of paper that says the same thing again? And who would attend in the future once your workbook starts making the rounds, copied or mimeographed for friends or sold under the table? That's the reason that you always leave the key points of your presentation **out** of the workbook. Its contents should be supplemental to what you say.

Workbooks can allow you to give, say, six hours of material in a four-hour program, by providing additional support and extension supplements in written form. That should be noted in the promotional writeups of the seminar, since it is a selling point. It should also be stated that workbooks are not sold separately.

Nothing irks participants more than a speaker who reads, word-for-word (and usually poorly), the contents of the workbook. It's best to integrate the workbook into the presentation early, explaining the parts that are for later reference and showing which pages you will explain in greater detail during the program.

Workbooks are invaluable when you want the participant to have a copy of the visuals used during the presentation. When your need goes beyond quick board or flipchart use, they allow you to provide the same visual so the listener can see and follow on a paper in hand. You may also want to project the same visual in the front of the room with an overhead or slide projector, to draw eye contact to your explanation.

Should you provide the workbook? In public seminars, some sponsors will prepare handouts for you. Then your problem will be making certain that they look good, are collated properly, and are available at the presentation. If you haven't sufficient certainty that the workbooks will be as you want them when you want them, it's best to prepare and provide them yourself.

At a contracted seminar, either the business will prepare and provide the workbooks or you will charge an additional fee for their preparation and provision, at commercial rates, though the actual charge is open to negotiation. If you include a flyer in the workbook telling how to purchase books, tapes, or other items by mail order, that will likely have to be excluded in workbooks for contracted seminars.

How much do workbooks cost? Figure about 5 cents a side if printed offset or duplicated in substantial quantity. Of the two, offset gives a sharper image. Use white or a soft light colored paper. Collating can be done economically by hand if the quantity is small, but consider machine collation for many-paged workbooks produced in quantity.

A cover is necessary. For an inexpensive seminar ($75 or less), a paper cover stapled on the front is acceptable. Typeset the title or use, with patience and a straightedge, press-on letters. A fancier cover -- probably with a plastic binding -- is appropriate for a higher priced program. When the fee is many hundreds of dollars, consider a cover with a spine into which a typeset insert can go with the name of the seminar, readable when the cover and contents are placed in a bookshelf. Copy on both sides of the paper is fine for inexpensive seminars. But switch to copy on one side only for costlier presentations. In fact, it will be the same basic workbook spread out and dolled up. The differences will be cosmetic.

Which brings us to the single most important point to be made about workbooks: they must add substantial value to your seminar. More important than the fact that participants expect to receive them, they must be sufficiently valuable to their owners that they won't want to part with them. Which means that their contents must be solid in conception and proper in form, with the spelling and grammar proofed, proofed again, and flawless. Long after you are forgotten, your workbook remains, with your name and phone number on front.

Simple, you say: get rid of the name and phone number and I can prepare workbooks in a more casual fashion. Sloppy workbooks? Fuzzy thinking? And without that name and phone number, who will call you for later consultation? Or attend other seminars you give? The workbook is part of the greater package: good ideas, good seminars, good support materials, good product sales, and a good future. Substitute excellent -- or poor -- for good and you get the idea.

Chapter 17

Promotion: General, "Free," and Paid

GENERAL PROMOTION

If nobody knows about your seminar, who will attend?

On the other hand, if it costs $2000 to advertise and you can expect to gross $1500 per day, why not just save the time and throw that $500 away? That is the dilemma of seminar promotion.

Don't despair, it's seldom that dire. The trick is to use common sense, be patient, and wade into the water slowly -- very slowly. There **are** sharks out there. But get wet. If you don't, how will you ever reach those gilded shores on the other side?

Why promote?

For two reasons: (1) to create an awareness of your seminar, and (2) to stimulate an interest in it.

Still, most advertising is expensive, and most of that doesn't earn back what it costs, much less a profit. So in this chapter we will focus on what does work for seminars, so you know what should be repeated while you seek supplemental ways to enhance its and your effectiveness.

What does promotional success depend upon?

In seminaring it depends upon (1) the sales potential of you and your seminar, (2) contacting the right market, and (3) finding the least expensive way to make that contact.

The (1) **sales potential of you and your seminar** has been at the core of this half-book thus far. Without a subject that others want to know more about, without a title that makes one want to register, and without a sense of the kind of audience that will respond to that subject and title, the seminar has no sales potential.

Unless you do. That is, unless enough people know you and have faith in what you do to attend your seminar, whatever it is called or costs and wherever it is held -- within reason! If you have that kind of public pull and it is properly promoted, then the topic, title, and market identity, if also properly tended to, will add that much more to your already sizable drawing power.

Few of the readers of these pages have that much personal draw. Most of us are known to our kin, our peers, our neighbors, and a half-dozen friends. So it is the seminar itself that must fill our halls, and only when we offer that program well and often will our names begin to attract additional registrants -- if promoted along with the topic and title to the right groups at the right rates!

Promotion alone is powerless to draw an honest quorum to a seminar that has no sales potential.

The success of your promotion lies far less in the advertising and promotional activities **per se** than in what you are selling, to whom, and how it is packaged.

If we assume, however -- what an asumption! -- that you have super contents in a fetching package, then you must (2) **contact the right market.** It's not enough to know that nose ring salesmen are bullish on your seminar, you must contact them. You must let them know what you are offering, how they will benefit, when it will be, how much it will cost -- in short, you must get something in their hands, or at least in their minds, about your presentation and why they should take part.

Naturally, it's better if you can remind them time and again, short of raising their dander. But more important, you must (3) **find the least expensive way to make that contact.** If it's really a bargain, then you will be able to repeat the reminder often.

You may have developed the best seminar ever devised, have your market pinpointed with devilish certainty, and never earn a dime. If it costs you $1000 to run a magazine ad, that's the only way you can reach the potential participants, and they are so poor that any fee over $10 eliminates them from attending, you must register 100 paying nearby respondents just to break even!

Or you could be sharing sweet harmony with oboe reedmakers, showing them how to quadruple their profits. You discover that one newsletter serves the entire industry and a full-page ad costs but $100. Moreover, your seminar costs $300 per person and there are 50 companies actively seeking new information. That's music to your ears. You can well afford that page several times, plus a mailing followed by a phone campaign.

The return after costs on every promotional dollar is usually the heart of your profit in seminaring.

Testing, Measuring, and Repeating What Works

Before discussing various forms of promotion, you want to evaluate every dollar spent against its results so that, over time, you have a clear gauge of what is worth the investment, what isn't, and where your money is best employed.

For example, say it costs you $100 for a display ad in the local newspaper, your seminar costs $50, and you draw two registrations from that ad. Is it worth your time to run that ad in the future? But if you drew seven registrations, it looks far more appealing!

To make this sort of evaluation you must keep accurate statistics and you must know what provoked the registrations. There are several ways to find this out. One, ask every person upon registration: "how did you first hear about this seminar?" and "what convinced you to register?" Explain that you are evaluating various means of promotion and that their answers will be much appreciated.

If they are responding to a written source, code each. In one ad you may include in the return address "Suite A." In another, "Suite B," and so on, with each advertisement and each form of submitted copy indicating a different suite. Other variations include adding a letter after the address or P.O. Box number, or even telling them who to contact: "Ask for Sally" or "Contact Pete." You keep a list of what each of these suites, letters, or names means and you can tell where they heard about your program.

For those responding by phone, you can indicate various extensions -- even though yours is a single phone. The caller asks for "extension 12," you thank him, put a tally by "12" on a sheet, and answer (in a slightly different pitch) "Extension 12, may I help you?" Or, as explained, you can have the respondent ask for a particular person, which is handled the same way. (Remember, if you are male and you always answer the phone, don't give female names in the ads!)

What's a "good" return on an advertising investment? There are too many variables to give you a concrete response, but we consider 3:1, $3 back for every $1 spent, the minimum to continue using that promotional form as the primary advertising tool. As a support or follow-up means, even 2:1 might be acceptable.

If you find a means that works well for you and a particular ad that draws, don't play around with it. Don't say, "it's working so well now just think how well it'd work if...." If it's accurate and working, leave it alone! Seek other means that draw as well or better before you alter that first copy. Keep at least one strong selling tool pulling full-time for you while you hunt for support (or even replacement) tools to add further strength to your promotion.

FREE PROMOTIONS

Paradoxically, the free forms of promotion often outdraw the paid, but you usually need both to cover the full spectrum of potential participants. Don't undervalue or overlook "freebies." Quite the reverse: spend the many hours and close attention to detail they require until you get this form of publicity learned and comprehensively covered.

Press Releases

A seminar is news, particularly to those who will benefit from what is said. So you must make its existence and its news hook(s) known to the media: newspapers (dailies, weeklies, monthlies, paid or hand-out), radio, TV, newsletters, magazines, company organs, trade publications, any printed circular read by potential participants.

Editors look for the timely element, something interesting, or something significant -- or all three. Garnish with human interest and the chances of its being used increase dramatically.

You must know some verities about newspaper life. One, they'd rather you'd buy an ad than run it as news. But if you do buy an ad, that doesn't guarantee that they will also use the news release!

Whether your copy is used depends on how newsworthy they feel the copy is, whether you or the event are local, how much rewriting is necessary (any will often get it set aside), if it is short, whether a photo accompanies the copy, how much other copy is fighting for space that day, and a dozen other variables, plus whim.

It's said that "one paragraph has twice the chance of being used as two, two has twice the chance of being used as three, and so on..." That's true. Full feature articles about seminars and seminar-givers are seen in print regularly, and you can submit them along with shorter versions, but always send the very short release in classical journalism style. The opening paragraph should contain the who, what, where, why, and when -- the five "w's" -- about the item.

Subsequent paragraphs decrease in importance. Ideally, releases contain a description of the seminar, the time, location, who sponsors

News Release and Tax Deduction Clause

NEWS RELEASE

COMMUNICATION UNLIMITED
P O BOX 1001
CARPINTERIA CALIFORNIA 93013

JUDY LITSINGER   *(805) 684-2469*

Release date: Sept. 1

"How To Set Up and Market Your Own Seminar" will be offered at the Sheraton Santa Barbara next Tuesday evening, Sept. 8, from 6-10 p.m., with pre-registration beginning at 5:30 in the Rincon Room.

"There's openings in this billion-dollar industry for all kinds of new seminars, particularly if they present 'how-to' information that helps companies or individuals meet their most pressing needs," says Gordon Burgett, who offers 110 seminars annually throughout the United States. "Here we show how to get started and going successfully."

Included in the program and the 24-page workbook given free to each participant is information about seminar organization, promotion, content, scheduling, fees, location, and product development/sale. For further information, call 684-2469.

– 30 –

TAX DEDUCTION CLAUSE

Tax Deduction for Educational Expenses Treasury regulation 1.162-5 permits an income tax deduction for educational expenses (registration fees and cost of travel, meals and lodging) undertaken to: (1) maintain or improve skills required in one's employment or other trade or business, or (2) meet express requirements of an employer or a law imposed as a condition to retention of employment, job status or rate of compensation.

it, and the most pertinent biographical information about the speaker. Editors trim from the bottom-up when editing to fit the copy into an available hole. News releases aren't O'Henry short stories. All the mystery is resolved by paragraph two. The rest adds depth, flavor, a quotation, a schedule.

Accuracy is essential: spellings, hours, dates. And keep it objective, without opinions or conclusions. Read other press releases to see how this is done if you are new to promotion.

This book contains an example of a typical news release, with **NEWS RELEASE** plainly visible on top, the company name (or source of information) and address below, and the name and phone number of a contact person for further information. Indicate when the item should be used (a date is better than "for immediate release"), followed by the copy double- or triple-spaced, with wide margins, particularly on the left. Use 8.5" x 11" white paper, one side only, and type with a black ribbon. At the end of the copy in the center of the page type either ### or "end." They mean the same thing.

To find the media in your area consult the telephone book, your library, or the current **Ayer Directory of Publications.** Releases to local dailies should arrive 7-10 days before the event; for weeklies or monthlies, a week before the deadline for the issue in question. Newsletters and magazines often have a lead time from 30-90 days before they reach the stands, while radio and TV need the copy at least a week before the day you want it used.

The release should be sent to the editor of the respective section where it would appear. For newspapers that is often the Feature Editor or Business Editor; for radio and TV, the News Editor or Features Editor; and for other media, just the Editor unless a specific subdivision is clearly more appropriate.

Particularly for newspapers, radio, and TV, call the respective editor 3-4 days after the mailing to ask whether the material arrived, if there are any questions you might answer for them, and whether they'd like to arrange an interview with the speaker by phone or before or after the seminar. (If you are inviting the media to attend the presentation as your guest, send a written invitation at least two weeks before the seminar, requesting an RSVP so the receptionist will admit them with a special packet of media material.)

Black and white **photos** (4 x 5's or 5 x 7's are fine) should accompany the copy sent to the print media in the city or area where the seminar will be given, in your hometown, or where you are as important as the program. A head and shoulder shot of you, or a fuller shot showing you speaking or presenting a program, are the kind most often used. A caption (a line to a paragraph long) should accompany every photo to identify those shown and give complete details of the event. Either tape this to the bottom of the photo or stick it to the back -- don't write or type on the back of the photo itself! Your name, address, and phone number should also be on each caption.)

Public Service Announcements are godsends if you are a non-profit group or are speaking to or for such an organization, even if you are charging a fee. Write or print those three words (or just P.S.A.) in large letters at the top of all forms of your press releases. If you are sponsored by a non-profit group, use their stationery or release form. Most media give preferential treatment to P.S.A. material. The only catch is that in some areas you must be approved by a local or regional board to qualify. So call a radio station, explain that you are preparing a P.S.A. release, are new to the area, and would they explain whether it needs an identification number from another organization -- and if so, which and how can you contact it? Then make that contact. Is it worth the effort? It can double your exposure.

Two different releases can be sent at the same time, one a paragraph or two, the other up to 250 words maximum. That way you can increase your chances that one of several will be chosen, depending upon the editor's space needs and other considerations.

Radio and TV stations can be sent the standard press releases as described or you can prepare special 3" x 5" cards in actual broadcast language, 50 words maximum, typed double-spaced.

Calendar Announcements

Newspapers generally include a "What's Happening in _____" section. While most of the items listed are public service in nature, prepare a separate release (titled CALENDAR ANNOUNCE-MENT) and mail it in with your others, on the chance that it may be used nonetheless. It should contain the same identification information as your other press releases, plus, in 50 words or less, the five "w's" and a follow-up phone number for further information. It is debatable whether the cost should be stated or whether the person should have to call, at which point the benefits could be described as they meet the caller's needs, thus increasing the chance of a sale.

Radio and TV stations also use a calendar format, so you can either send them a standard release or a 3 x 5 card as described above.

Talk Shows

An appearance on a widely-broadcast radio or TV talk show can increase your seminar audience remarkably and it's all but free to arrange. Even when an appearance doesn't yield a bigger crowd the first time around, the exposure brings long range dividends by enhancing your perceived expertise.

Seek this form of promotion. Make a list of all talk shows in the area, when they are heard, and who produces them. Send a media packet to each producer. This should include a topic sheet, a list of where you have appeared before, sample questions, and a letter of presentation.

A one-page topic sheet explains what you will talk about, your credentials and experience, and why the subject and what you have to say about it would interest the listeners. Include a short introduction of yourself as you want it read on the air. In the introduction focus particularly on those things you have done related to that topic that will impress the listeners.

If you've not been on a talk show before, don't mention it. If your exposure has been modest, list it in the presentation letter. But if it's extensive, a separate sheet should indicate -- starting with the most recent and moving backward -- the name and host of the program, the call letters of the station, the city/state, and the date of broadcast. Also mention if the show was a call-in.

Sample questions can get you the invitation. Include 15-20 sharp questions, the kind that a bright, somewhat dubious host would ask: to the point, challenging, bottom-line, no-nonsense. Just send the questions. Many a producer or host will have you on to hear the answers!

Finally, your letter of presentation. This is the door-opener. If it is amateurish, sloppy, too cute, or dull it's unlikely that the producer will bother to read the attachments. Catch the producer's interest in the opening paragraph by presenting your topic in a different way. Then tell who you are and why you are talking about it. Cite the attachments, which reinforce these points, and indicate that you will follow up this letter with a telephone call in so many days.

If you have recently published a book, send information about it with either a copy or an invitation to send a copy, if interested. If you've had an article recently in print about the subject, send a sample. Reviews or testimonials can accompany the published items or can be sent with the letter of presentation, appropriately cited.

Persist. Telephone. Send anything else the producer requests. And when an appearance date is scheduled, reconfirm it. Then arrive far enough in advance to allay your travel jitters, compose yourself, review your sample questions, smile, relax, and talk with the same sharpness, sensitivity, and humor you use at your seminars. How can you go wrong?

If you are to appear on television, avoid white shirts, polka dots, or screaming plaids. Lift your head slightly when you speak, smile when appropriate, scratch sparingly, relax, don't squint, and stay seated when you think your segment has ended until somebody says it's time to rise! The rest is easy.

Remind the host to plug your seminar (or book) during the break before the final segment. Mention your activities or services when it is proper. But let you, your knowledge and experience, and your articulation do most of your selling. If people like what they hear (and see), all you have to do is let them know how they can buy more good things from that source.

PAID PROMOTION

Try all of the freebies that fit your topic -- the price is right and the yield is often high. But you can't stop there. Rare is the public seminar that doesn't need paid promotion as well. The most common forms of paid promotion involve advertisements in newspapers, magazines, and other print media; spots on the radio or TV; posters; and brochures or flyers for both direct and mail distribution.

Let's discuss each as it would apply to a self-sponsored public seminar, then summarize later how that would differ when the seminar is sponsored by another group, particularly a college or university.

For in-house or customized programs the promotion is provided by the contractor, with your promotion mainly directed at getting the client's interest and then getting the contract signed. That is done directly -- mail, phone, interview -- without any of the freebie or paid promotional means described in this section of the book.

Newspaper, Magazine, and Print Media Advertising

When you ask a new seminar-giver how he or she will draw registrants to a program, the usual response is, "I'll put an ad in the paper!" Alas, if it were that easy!

Print media advertising is rarely the best way to sell seminars. Often it doesn't work at all.

These are the problems with print media ads:

(1.) They are very expensive.
(2.) They work best when repeated over and over.
(3.) They are usually unattractive.
(4.) They are usually buried among other ads.
(5.) The media is rarely directed at a particular reader.

Of the five, the last provides the best clue as to when print media works for seminars and when it doesn't. Use your home newspaper as an example. It is written for anybody over about 10 who picks it up and reads it. But your seminar is directed at retiring nurses, beet growers, budding insurance executives, or people who want to get rich quick. In the first three cases you must spend money to let 99% of the populace read your ad just so the other 1% -- the retiring nurses, beet growers, and so on -- will also see it.

In the last case, where you want to attract anybody eager to get rich quick, the newspaper may be the most effective and least expensive way to get the message to the greatest number of potential registrants. Therefore, consider general print media when you want to attract registrants from a wide range of backgrounds and interests. Or when you can't zero in on your limited market any other way.

You are an example of a person who might be best reached by print media. Potential seminar-givers come from all fields; are male or female; some rich, some poor; many degreed, others more street-wise than book-filled. Yet only a few from each discipline want to set up and market their own seminars. So an ad in a magazine for psychologists or a newsletter for I.R.A. consultants will attract a handful of brave souls with bright minds. But an ad in a widely-circulated newspaper will bring dozens. (A write-up in a college extended education catalog that is widely distributed will do the same.)

Most seminars, however, are specifically set up to appeal to a tightly-identified market: again, the retiring nurses, beet growers, and budding insurance executives. Usually brochures or flyers are the best means of contacting these markets, but where the print media is also tightly-focussed consider ads in print as well as flyers. For retiring nurses, for example, an excellent vehicle for advertising might be newspapers, newsletters, and magazines written and distributed to nurses.

If you decide to promote through the print media, determine which publications are directed at your potential participants, then study their rates, circulation, ad sizes, and deadlines. This information is found in the Standard Rate and Data Services publications in your library, or you can request a rate sheet (which includes this information) from the newspapers and magazines themselves.

Check past copies of the actual publications to see how often others used them to advertise seminars or similar offerings. Study those ads. Are they classified or display ads? In what section do they appear? How could you improve them to better sell your own program?

How does newspaper advertising differ from newsletters and magazines for seminars? Setting the rates aside, newspapers usually have a far shorter lead time than newsletters or magazines. An ad submitted early today can appear in tomorrow afternoon's newspaper. The others are published far less often so ads must be submitted weeks, more often months, before they appear. Newspapers (and sometimes newsletters) will usually set the ad from an oral description or rough written design at no additional cost (although it is better to submit an ad that is ready to use, called "camera-ready," so you can control its appearance). Magazines want ads "camera-ready."

The real quandry is whether the ad you run will bring in enough registrations to make offering your seminar profitable. Pay attention to the ad itself. Does it say how the participant will benefit, that is, why he or she should attend? Does it make sense? Is it clear? Are all the details accurate, all the "w's" included? Did you include a phone number or address for a response?

Within reason, the bigger the ad and the more often you run it the likelier it is that each time you will find more people eager to sign up. However, an advertisement a third of a page, high and on the right side, will draw almost as well as a full page, and much more than four or five days in a newspaper, starting 7-10 days in advance, and your response percentage usually starts dropping. So be frugal at the outset. Run as much ad space as often as you think you need and can afford for as long as you think makes sense, and see what happens. Don't mortgage the children; use surplus funds. Then build around those numbers for future programs -- or seek a more profitable mode of promotion. There are no certainties. You must experiment, but wisely and with fiscal caution.

Radio and TV

Too expensive and too widely broadcast for all but a handful of seminars. And if you're going to do it right, it costs more than you can recoup to produce the ads professionally.

Yet as a secondary or support form of advertising it can't be summarily dismissed. A relatively small city had one classical music station. Each night it ran popular evening programs of string music, concerts, and opera or ballet. A seminar called "Writing Travel Articles That Sell" was advertised on six 30-second spots, one a night, for a presentation on the seventh day, a Sunday afternoon. For every dollar spent the ad brought in $3.20 in registrations, plus B.O.R. sales. The premise was simple: those with the money and time to travel probably listened to classical music. A $120 risk brought a $384-500 return. (But when the same scheduling was tried with a different seminar it brought in precisely what it cost! You have to test.)

Here's another problem with radio. How many people really listen? Of those, how many will have a pencil and paper on hand to write down the phone number? And how many will remember what that phone number is for an hour later?

Posters

Fine for punk rock concerts, college gatherings, and company in-house meetings but inappropriate for seminars. The exception is home-town programs where you know the magic sites where posters draw. In one town in California any event of worth will considerably improve its attendance with a poster taped inside the window next door to the post office. But otherwise focus elsewhere.

Flyers or brochures

These are the difference between feast and famine for most seminar-givers, who start with a tightly-focussed, accessible market, then fashion a seminar to meet its need. Finally, they put something in the hands of those in that market that produces registrations. That something is a flyer, used here generically to include brochures.

Tightly-focussed means that the likely participant is clearly iden-tified within a narrow range of people, by vocation, avocation, desire, skill, age, etc. Accessible usually means that a mailing list, or many, exists through which these specific kinds of people can be contacted. The need the seminar meets can be unique to this market, universal but explained in terms of this market, or little known to this market but sold to it because of the benefits it can offer.

The flyer is the pivotal element between the idea and the semi-nar. It converts the idea into needs, benefits, the five "w's," your credentials, ways to register, sometimes a schedule, the cost, and a description that makes the reader want to sign up yesterday -- twice!

Format

Some things must appear on flyers; the rest is artwork, creativity, and the further traces of the genius seminar-givers need to succeed.

It must include the seminar's **title** in very large letters, and **your name** (or the speaker's) in smaller letters nearby, unless the name is really what is bringing the crowd, then reverse the sizes.

It must answer the **who, what, where, why, when** -- and **how** -- of the presentation. The what, why, and how are the description. How long must the description be? Your description must be long enough to describe the seminar to the reader.

In that description or elsewhere on the flyer tell why the reader would benefit from attending. Nothing is more important than that. If the reader doesn't see quickly and clearly the advantages to be gained from attending and paying, the rest of the copy will go unread or at least will not lead to a registration. Not all of the benefits need be logical or pecuniary, either. Basic drives, impulse, imitation, a hope for immortality through creative recognition, some of the reasons for attending a seminar and the ways that benefits are perceived will occur to and attract participants only if they are stated or implied in the copy itself.

Most **benefits** are far less mystical. People attend seminars to get ahead, acquire fame or money, perfect a skill, get promoted, learn a new technique or how to write a sonnet or paint eggs, to look better, lose weight, do something different, meet a mate, ... Tell why a person will be better for having taken part.

Describe yourself (or the speaker): a compact **biographical sketch.** Focus on your credentials and experience as they relate to the topic. The reader wants to know why he should pay to hear you. What have you done that makes your advice worth the time and money? So respond briefly. A photo (tell the printer you want a half-tone) of you reduces the mystery -- if you are attractive and your age is a selling factor. Use a head and shoulders shot or one of you giving the seminar or doing what you lecture about. Make certain you are dressed appropriately: tie and coat for business, fishing togs for fishing, etc.

Testimonials are worth including if they are strong, clear, believably positive, and unambiguous. Some won't believe them anyway, of course, but it will be the difference for others between attending or just thinking about it. Each testimonial should be written and signed by the person and should include a note permitting you to use it for promotional purposes. To add greater legitimacy you can print after the comments the person's name, age (with their agreement), vocation, and city of residence.

How do you get testimonials? People will write you later, usually seeking information, in which kind comments will be stated. You can send a copy of that letter back with your reply, with a permission form, a self-addressed stamped envelope, and a request to use the indicated part for promotion. Or you can put testimonial forms on a table at the seminar and, in a light vein, suggest that if anybody is about to swoon with enthusiasm they might want to transfer their elation and good will to that form and leave some of it behind! Or 101 other methods.

Anticipate the reader's questions and try to answer as many as fit the style of your flyer in the copy. But don't use a question-answer format, which looks too amateurish.

Make certain that the reader knows how to **register** (by phone, in person, return the form), how to **pay** (check or credit card), and when the **deadlines** are for signing up and/or receiving a discount.

If he can register by phone, can he call collect? Do you have a 800 number? Few will actually do the former; the latter makes sense if it's from out of state and the seminar cost is $100 or more. Can he sign up now or at the door? Is that clear? Or must he return the dotted part of the flyer with payment or a credit card number? Can he sign up only at the door? (Until you know your field from experience it probably makes most sense to encourage phone and mail-in registrations, but indicate on the flyer that "registration gladly accepted at the door, space permitting."

Seminar participants are generally excellent credit risks so personal checks represent scant danger. Credit cards, though, should be checked on advance registrations before confirmation is sent. It is doubly prudent to verify the actual card numbers and expiration date before selling B.O.R. items against a credit card. Mastercharge and VISA are all you need for most public seminars, but if you speak to the monied fringe you should add American Express and Diner's Club too. Cash is also acceptable -- U.S. cash.

It's a wise sales technique to give a person a reason for registering in advance by a certain date. Set a week or 10 days prior to the seminar as a deadline (but don't quibble if they miss it by a day or two and still claim the premium). A fee discount works best -- 10%, $25 -- something that is clearly of value. Or a copy of your book, if it's related to the topic. Or even the total seminar fee returned in cash, chosen for one participant during the seminar (from a hat) among those who have registered by the cut-off date.

Some other items to include, where applicable: your cancellation/refund policy, meals (are they included or will you point out eating places nearby?), can they stay at the site of the seminar or will you assist in finding lodging, will you provide transportation, a phone number for additional information, and a tax deductibility clause.

Tone and Appearance of the Flyer

The **tone** of the flyer should be properly positive, even a bit hyped -- but totally honest. That is, it must read like other flyers. It must impress the reader for its clarity and professional writing skill.

The **appearance** must follow suit, for you will be judged by how the flyer looks before it is read. If it's crooked, smudged, and printed on toilet paper, the flyer could promise salvation for $1 and scarcely a person would bother to read it. After all, who wants to waste time listening to a person who doesn't even have his advertising together?

So the flyer should be pleasing to look at, professional in appearance, typeset or typed with various fonts, printed on paper of some substance, and folded cleanly (if mailed).

Find a half-dozen or more flyers about seminars similar to yours. Pick from them the features or style you want on yours. Lay out a rough sketch of how your flyer would look when printed. Then take this to a print shop to get a bid for the number that you want produced.

Printers' prices for the same job vary widely so take the terms in your first bid, draw up a model bid request, and submit it to 6 or 8 more printers. Select the best bid, then determine whether you can provide camera-ready copy or the printer should set the type and paste it up. The latter costs more but in leiu of experience and the proper equipment it probably makes sense early in the game so your first flyers look appropriately professional.

At the outset confine yourself to one color (white paper with black ink, for example), plus variations with shading or, at most, two colors with shading, on a good grade paper. Slick paper costs more but holds a better photo. Vellum or a soft-touch paper is impressive for the price. Let your printers show you papers and explain the shading. Your task is to create a flyer that looks expensive but costs little.

Learn pasteup and layout skills early in your seminaring career. Someone else's seminar about flyer or brochure preparation at a nearby college, supplemented by Walter Graham's **Complete Guide To Pasteup**, will steer you to the right tools and supplies. Not only will that save you plenty of money, you will develop a better eye for all facets of visual and copy promotion.

Mailing your flyer

Since the reason you decided to prepare flyers was to put them in the hands of your target market, now you must either deliver them -- what more is there to say? -- or mail them.

To mail them you need a mailing list. You can find appropriate lists through the Standard Rate and Data Services publications in your library, you can buy them through list brokers, or a local mailing house (see your yellow pages under "mail" and "mailing lists") can buy them for you. It costs the same.

If the number of flyers you will mail is small, say 500 or less, you may wish to buy pressure-sensitive or self-adhesive labels and apply them yourself. Above 500 or 1000 it makes more sense to let the mailing house order chesire labels (they cost less but need a special machine to use), apply them, and zip sort and mail the flyers.

For 200 or more of like items you can send them bulk rate, which is roughly half the price of first class. Currently it costs $80 to use the bulk rate service, $40 annually and $40 to get an indicia number. To save $40 of that most mailing houses will allow you to use their indicia number, as long as you pay the annual fee. So by letting them pick up the time-consuming labelling, sorting, and mailing tasks at a low cost you also save money three ways: on the indicia number, by using bulk rate, and by using chesire labels.

How many flyers must you mail to reap a profitable harvest of listeners? You must find that out, frankly, by testing. Figure that each mailed flyer will cost from 25-30 cents apiece by the time it is in a recipient's hand. Using a working figure of 2% for registration response, you can calculate based on your charge for the seminar how many you must send out to pass into the black. But many do not get even a 2% return, particularly for programs with high fees. Follow-up seminars, on the other hand, should be closer to 5%. So the number is an unknown until you offer a program a few times.

Again, don't produce a million flyers for a new program. Test with a reasonable number: 500, 1000, 2000. Put your attention into the flyer itself. Learn the process so that you can fine tune it intelligently later.

Finally, run extra flyers so you can distribute them to any group, person, organization, club, society, or person that you think would be interested in attending. That includes your family, friends, and peers. Hand them out freely, encouraging people to share the flyers with others who may be interested.

How does this differ for sponsored seminars?

Using the college/university-sponsored programs as an example, as we've said, they normally keep a percentage of your earnings in exchange for listing your seminar in the catalog, providing other promotional services, supplying a room, and handling pre-registration.

If the catalog is sent to enough people and the write-up is decently placed you may not need additional promotion, other than telling friends and others interested in the program when and where it is being offered. In fact that's why it's an excellent idea to learn the trade by booking through schools, to reduce the risks of promotional costs.

Unfortunately, most colleges are poor at providing "additional promotion." That usually means a press release sent out if they remember. So there you might bolster their activities, after checking to make sure you are not overlapping. In particular, set up your own radio/TV talk show spots or interviews. If you sell products, consider a flyer to your own mailing list that both sells your items and advertises your seminars. (Provide the day, date, hours, title, and extended education phone number so the recipient registers directly through the school.)

You are your own best promotion

You are your best advertising. Put your enthusiasm, your planning, your drive, and your articulation in action, on paper, and in motion through friends. Let everybody know. Keep a hard eye on expenses. Study everything you see in print or on radio and TV to see how others are doing it and how you can improve. By your third seminar you'll be a walking veteran. If you hustle, plan, and economize enough in the beginning to last three!

Chapter 18

Costs

Offering seminars costs money. Yet if you can earn sufficiently more than the costs to justify the time and effort, then they are worth the doing, even if you disregard the many other benefits that sharing information with others also brings.

It is hard to categorize those costs because many are personal. Others, mostly in time, defy clear monetary equation. So it might be simpler to list the most common expenses to see how they relate to seminar-giving. As usual, we shall focus on the costs incurred in offering your own seminars, with a special section explaining how those would differ for in-house or customized programs.

PREPARATION AND HOME COSTS

Feasibility Study

The costs here are both in research time and the related expenses of finding materials, travel to libraries and other seminars, registration fees, food and lodging expenses, the purchase of magazines and journals, reproduction costs of articles, and so on.

Office

Most seminars start as secondary moneymakers offered on an occasional evening or weekend. The "office" is a kitchen table or desk in the den, a telephone, a cardboard box with folders, and a general-duty home typewriter.

There's no reason to abandon that any quicker than is necessary. When seminaring becomes more central to the family income, the necessary support items will become obvious: an actual working space, a file cabinet, a phone at hand, perhaps a better typewriter. Later, if needed, comes the full office, the computer and letter-quality printer, phone-answering device, etc. Don't invest heavily in such items until the enterprise is well launched.

When do you move the office out of your home? Some never do. Others find the distractions too much to bear; still others have difficulty disciplining themselves except on "other ground." That decision is yours and is based on so many personal factors they can't be isolated here. In other businesses the appearance of the house, literally and/or figuratively, and the amount of foot traffic make home use impractical. In speaking, neither rules out home use. More important, the costs of an outside office, usually with a staff to manage it, are sizable and eat into usually scarce starting capital probably better spent on basics and promotion, at least at the outset. Again, invest in a separate office when it would clearly improve your profits and productivity. Until then, focus on your seminar.

Staff

When do you bring in somebody else to help carry the load? When it's necessary, you can afford it, and you will use that freed time to do other things more beneficial to your seminar-giving. Thus, like an office, you start slowly and let necessity be the guide.

For simple labor -- collating, addressing, zip sorting -- hire kids, seniors, cousins, anybody responsible who is eager to pick up short-job cash. If you are adept at basic office skills, teach these to a high school or college student (or a mother with children in school) eager to gain part-time experience. They can handle your mail, product fulfillment, and simple bookkeeping.

Then, when your activities grow to the point that more responsible, part-day or full-day coverage is necessary, look for a secretary with skills in the public relations area who can both assume the other jobs (or supervise those already handling them) and can directly produce the most time-consuming of all office work: promotion. Later, should you grow to the point of needing a full staff, this secretary is then fully prepared to move into the office manager's position.

But in the beginning keep it simple, hire only as necessary, work on a contract basis whenever possible (to avoid the taxes and additional costs incurred with regular employees), and expand only as your income, actual or highly probable, expands. Which in the meantime means long hours for you (and sometimes your family), but in turn has the beneficial effect of forcing you to learn every aspect of the business side of speaking from the bottom up.

Printing

You should learn the basics of layout, pasteup, and simple reproduction and printing. An excellent primer is Walter Graham's **Complete**

Guide To Pasteup (2nd ed., 1980; P.O. Box 369, Omaha, NE 68101), mentioned in the section about promotion. You must also become aware of the holdings and services of local stationery/art supply stores and printers.

You will need workbooks or seminar handouts as well as promotional material early in your seminaring. Most workbooks or handouts are typed material, sometimes with art added, inside a better-looking cover, stapled. Small or quick-print shops can handle those demands. Only the more elaborate promotional material or books will require greater graphics skills and equipment.

So what you need is a typewriter that cuts clear copy. Different sized or faced type adds welcome variety to the printed page. You can rent an IBM or similar quality typewriter to prepare the masters, and with reduction copiers available at many fast-print shops you can produce a wide variety of attractive workbooks at a minimal expense.

Word processors are time-savers if you self-publish books or write extensively for publication, but they aren't necessary early in your seminaring career. And why buy a copier when it costs so little to reproduce your needs locally?

Stationery and Supplies

You need stationery -- paper and envelopes -- plus invoices (if you sell a product) with your name and address, or your company's, cleanly printed on each. On the stationery the printing should be identical in style and color. At least it must be business-like, neat, and professionally prepared. If you are contacting extended education directors at colleges, you needn't spend a fortune on stationery. But if you are working the corporate level, or dealing in a structure where such externals are important, put money into its appearance.

Do you need a logo and many matched colors? Only when you're trying to impress the highest rollers is it even worth considering. If not, you can usually do just fine by dealing with a local print shop and finding examples among their samples to use as a model for your stationery. Or you can contact The Drawing Board (800-527-9530), NEBS (800-252-9226), or a similar supply house to request catalogs that show integrated stationery, window envelopes, and invoices that will get you going at a reasonable price.

As for other supplies, buy in small quantities until you are certain of future needs and quality/cost. Keep office costs to a minimum so you can put the money where it is more needed at the outset.

108

Phone

If you have an office you need a phone. But if you're at home it makes no sense to rush out and install a business line until the business is a reality. The problem is more one of keeping the kids off the line and getting the messages straight. A second family phone usually takes care of the kids, and a bit of telephone education gently given to your spouse (or home office helper), plus a pen and paper at hand, go a long way in handling the messages. Better yet, a questionnaire with the opening dialog and follow-up information might be placed nearby. Type up a master and make copies, changing the questionnaire as needed.

Unless you're selling a lower-priced product to a mass-market audience, and then it is questionable, you needn't invest in an 800 number. Those interested in higher-priced seminars will pay for the call.

Bookkeeping and Taxes

This is far simpler than it sounds. All you must prove to Uncle Sam at tax time is (1) you are in business, (2) how much money your business brought in (or is promised for items or services sold), (3) how much money your business spent (or owes for items or services bought), (4) who paid your business and whom your business paid, and (5) how much the business owes him for tax. The state needs the same information.

You are in business because you say you are and you are doing business-like things in a business-like way. You don't need a license to own a business **per se.** You are a single proprietor, in a partnership, or are part of a corporation. Let's focus on the first. At tax time you complete Schedule C, adjust your 1040 accordingly, and that is how you account for your business taxes. Your income may cause you to have to file estimated tax forms instead of a W-4, and pay quarterly. Read **Small Business Tax Guide** published by the IRS for more details.

If you sell a product, you must pay your state a sales tax. This is usually done quarterly, but check the appropriate agency for details. The amount you owe can be calculated from the tally you keep of the money received from the sales.

Therefore in (2) you keep a close tally of the items sold, the tax collected (if they are products), and those who purchased your goods or services but have yet to pay. Seminars given to schools often fall for a while in the last category: given but unpaid, or "accounts receivable." You need pay tax on them only when the money is actually received.

As for expenditures (3), keep a receipt of every expense (except regular meals or incidentals where receipts aren't given). Note those without receipts in a booklet you keep with you, and for driving keep a notebook in the glove compartment where you tally each business trip taken, the date, the purpose, and the odometer reading or mileage.

Post these regularly on your ledger sheets, and ultimately on your Schedule C. The receipts (or cancelled checks) and notations prove that you actually spent the money -- and how. In the beginning if your expenses exceed your income -- in fact, if there is no income at all -- you can continue to claim the expenses. A rough rule-of-thumb used by the IRS is that you must show a profit in at least two of five years or you will be forced to prove that your "business" isn't really a hobby. (For a hobby you must pay the costs!)

Do you need a bookkeeper? Certainly not in the earliest days. Nor should you let a tax period pass without preparing your own forms, to get a firm grasp on how the system works. But later, once you understand the process and how to function within it, you may prefer to pay another to keep track of the daily accounting or the occasional tax filing.

The other requisites, (4) and (5), will be taken care of with careful recordkeeping and familiarization with the forms to file with the federal and state governments.

Licenses

There's no federal license for seminaring. Some states require either that a fee be paid or certification be granted, but they are in the vast minority and they generally exempt programs given at or to licensed educational institutions. Check the Departments of Education.

More common are the cities that require a business license to offer public seminars within their boundaries. And the states that require collection and payment of state tax on products sold at your presentations. How do you find out? You can contact the city and state, check with the local Chamber of Commerce, ask others who have recently offered a similar program in that city/state, or wait for them to find you.

Promotion

Rather than repeat much of what is said in the chapter about promotion, let's reinforce the fact that promotional costs, unless you speak through extended education programs, may well be the largest expense of all. In fact, it is wholly imaginable that as much as 60-70% of the budget can be spent here.

That's the "catch 22" of seminaring. In the beginning, if you offer public seminars, you need the most and best promotion, and since you are still a novice at extracting the best product and stretching it the farthest from the best controlled expenses, you are likely to pay too much for too little. Worst yet, your promotion may not attract enough registrants to even offer the seminar! You may spend two-thirds of your precious venture capital and reap no reward.

Thus, like all other costs, it seems prudent to reverse that order by offering seminars where you can exchange part of the income for others' promotion, letting them risk the pre-presentation costs on the hope that your topic will draw a response great enough to pay those expenses and leave a profit for you and them. That's where finding a sponsor early in your career makes sense. And where the college/university systems are ideal for most.

You test your programs and learn your skills at their risk. Then, if appropriate, you move into the public or corporate arenas, building your own promotional skills and augmenting your promotional budget around seminars that have a proven track record elsewhere. You are then selling a known product and you are a recognized speaker. You keep your financial feet in the sponsored camp while dipping a toe elsewhere. When the new waters prove profitable and to your liking you increase your own promotional activities to the level needed to achieve your new goals.

Postage

The biggest savings in this area comes with a bulk mail permit. If you are sending 200 or more like items they can be mailed for about half the first-class rate -- even lower if you are a non-profit organization (by intention!). Your post office will give you the details. Or if you are mailing 500 or more items, seriously consider using a mailing service. They will label, zip sort, and send the missives at far less in time-dollars than you can match, and most will let you use their bulk mail indicia, saving you $40 of the $80 cost for the bulk mail permit. (You must still pay $40 annually.)

If you send your products by mail order be sure to learn about special rates for books, tapes, printed matter, and library destinations. Compare U.P.S. rates and service with the Post Office on larger items, and also check the postal insurance rates for objects over about $50 in value. The loss rate on insured items is remarkably lower -- and recoverable.

SITE OR TRAVEL COSTS

Audio-visuals/Microphone

As soon as your seminars are on solid footing and your budget allows, you should buy your own audio-visual machinery and your own microphone and amplification system. In the meantime, you must trust (the word is used with trepidation) what is provided or you can rent what you need.

Overhead projectors are excellent, if they are silent, for programs that require daily alteration of the material being shown. Slide projectors work well too, particularly if the speaker can manually control the changing of the slides. Remember to purchase and bring extra bulbs and cords.

Microphones only add to the presentation when they amplify clearly what is said, so the amplification and speaker(s) should be of the same high quality as the microphone itself. If you must use your hands in the presentation, a clip-on microphone should be tried. Otherwise a hand-held type with ample cord extension allows you to roam about and be heard everywhere at all times.

Attire

You must dress the part when you offer seminars. It needn't be tux and tails, which would indeed look odd at a program about horseshoeing. But it must show you as successful in the field as well as clean, neat, and visually appealing. Remember, the participants can judge you only from what they see and hear. All follow-up benefits come from that judgement, so what they see must reinforce your sterling oral presentation. A minimum: dress a shade better than the participants for the task at hand. Yet if it's a mass market gathering, don't make the listeners feel unduly self-conscious by your sartorial splendor.

Transportation

After promotion, transportation may be your greatest expense. It will consistently be your greatest concern, for the best laid plans are for naught if you can't reach the seminar site before the participants have left!

If you travel primarily by car, yours must be in dependable shape at all times, with a standby when it's not. (Local car rentals will do in a pinch, even Rent-a-Wrecks if the site is nearby. But a family or friend's second car is better, rentable for a short term in an emergency.) The size of car needed will be determined by the amount of B.O.R. items, workbooks, and clothes you must carry, which in turn will be dictated by the number of seminars on your tour.

This is even more complicated if part of your trip is made by air. Not only must you have a reliable travel agency and a solid grasp of airport parking, connections, and handling, you must coordinate the sending of all the vital materials so that they and you arrive at the same place at the same time. The alternative is to send part of the items ahead as freight, addressed to a specific person whose name will be given to you by the facilities manager at the hotel/motel where the seminar will be held.

Lodging

Nothing can sour a trip faster than arriving at a hotel/motel that has no vacancy. That is usually avoidable by receiving written confirmations months in advance -- six months or more during a resort season or a travel holiday. For the other 10% who overbook and won't honor your confirmation, have a standby motel in the area, with confirmation also secured. (Don't forget to inform that original hotel/motel, through a letter to the president of the chain or the chairman of the board, why you won't be staying there in the future: facts, copies of confirmation, etc. Likely they will rectify the problem in your favor, positively and permanently.)

Only when you will be entertaining in your room or inviting consulting clients back is the setting of particular importance. If you are offering your seminars at a hotel/motel you would likely stay there, at a discount (if not a free room) arranged through the facilities manager.

Otherwise, where you stay is up to you. Proximity to the seminar site will reduce travel time and tension, but don't forget your own needs: a restaurant nearby for a post-program meal, a beach or park if outdoor exercise is part of your daily routine, a first-floor room if you keep your supplies inside, a sauna or pool....

Food

Seminars invariably distort your regular eating schedule, so it is up to you to devise a nutritive, energy-infusing system of your own. Evening seminars, from 6-10, require you to be there by 5, so you must eat supper by 4. Or, if you are one of those who must speak without a full stomach, an eight-hour fast will have you starving by the time you leave at 11 -- the very hour that many restaurants close! Daytime seminars are just as vexing.

One solution is to keep a supply of fruit and fixable provisions in your room, to be eaten around one or two major but oddly-timed meals a day. Fast-food havens are another solution, particularly for a quick, solitary lunch squeezed between morning and afternoon gatherings. There is no universally applicable solution. Just don't lodge miles from the closest morsel.

Drinks

Just a word here. Alcohol and sharp presentations don't mix. If you drink, do it as a reward for a job well done, not a primer for the pump. And do it in moderation: there's always another seminar or client tomorrow!

Cleaning

If you're on the road for days or weeks and must keep your clothes to a minimum, usually because you're flying, drip-dry clothes are a godsend. One-day cleaning is a blessing too. With a quick stop at the laundromat, the three should keep you going for years.

Location

If you are offering seminars on your own you will almost always need a location at which they can be held. This is discussed in the chapter about "Location." Suffice it to say that the location cost is prorated against the anticipated number of participants and is collected in the registration fee.

Registration

When staging your own seminars you must provide a means for the interested to register. This is usually done before the presentation, with the interested either sending the fee by mail to a designated address, registering by phone at an indicated number, or calling for information but registering by mail. Sometimes on-site registration is the only requirement. Others encourage early registration, often giving a fee discount or free product if done by a set date, but will accept at-the-door "late" registration.

Your expense comes in providing a contact person to be available by phone, the paperhandler for the mail registrations, and the collector at the registration itself.

If you use your own office staff for phone and mail contact, fine -- except where it's a toll call away. In which case an 800 number is almost mandatory. An alternate method is to use another, local office in the city where the seminar is being held, for a fee or in exchange for services or seminar seats. You can even run a classified ad for a local stay-at-home who will handle at least the phone element.

The on-site collector before the actual seminar can be from one of those sources or can be hired on a one-day basis from Manpower or a similar group. The same person should handle the B.O.R. sales after (and perhaps during the breaks) of the seminar. Be certain that person arrives an hour before the seminar is scheduled to begin so you can fully explain the duties and can coach him or her on how to answer the most common questions.

None of this is an issue at in-house, customized, or college/university bookings. In the third case most of the participants pre-register with the school, and you can usually handle at-the-door walk-ins. Or you can dragoon a participant to handle the registration (and even B.O.R. sales) in exchange for a product from your display table!

IN-HOUSE AND CUSTOMIZED PROGRAMS

Many of the costs for in-house and customized programs differ from those incurred when the seminars are given in public.

For example, promotional costs to attract the participants are totally eliminated, which is normally the bulk of your risk capital. For in-house programs the sponsor provides the participants; in the customized programs you simply provide the program and the sponsor (usually) makes arrangements for its presentation to its participants.

In both cases most of your initial costs are spent in approaching the sponsor for a sales interview. Thus your focus is on the feasibility study, stationery, accompanying materials, and telephoning. Later, an interview secured, you may wish to present a proposal, with a copy of handout materials and perhaps an indication of the audio-visuals to be used. Finally, your costs will be determined by the contract signed, and will be directly related to the fulfillment of its obligations, plus any follow-up sales costs that emanate from it.

COLLEGE/UNIVERSITY SEMINARS

The initial costs of offering seminars at colleges and universities is almost identical to that for in-house and customized programs, since you must convince the director of the extended education (or similar) program to include your offering(s) in the coming schedule.

This can frequently be done by mail, which reduces the cost of personal visits to distant locations. Yet after your seminars have been booked you generally incur many of the same expenses you would if you booked the program alone, with the exception of the room rental, pre-registration, and promotion through the catalog or bulletin, which are provided by the institution in exchange for a portion of your income.

Whether you wish to supplement the institution's promotion depends upon whether that additional expense will ultimately be more lucrative to you. If you are speaking at many schools on an extended tour and you have products for sale that can be purchased whether or not the person attends your seminar(s), you may wish to circulate a flyer advertising both the seminars and your products, letting the profits from the sale of the latter pay for the flyer and mailing costs while the additional seminar registration income provides the reason for the time and skills expenditure.

Chapter 19

Evaluations

The best way to find out how well your seminars are being received is to ask the recipients, and the best way to do that is with written evaluations.

If you are booking through an institution or have a sponsor, they will often devise their own evaluations. These seem to fall into two categories: either written in such a way that they garner positive responses (to be sent up the administrative ranks) or they attempt to discover how and where the participant heard of the seminar. Seldom do they focus on its content or your delivery.

In those cases you can add your own evaluation to theirs and distribute both, though the participants may grumble at the paperwork and some will fill in neither.

Often, though, your own evaluation sheet can simply be distributed with your workbook and product flyer(s). If it's not too long or complicated it can be filled in during the seminar and left. That is far preferable to asking the participant to mail it back later. (In the latter case a return rate of 20% is excellent, even if you provide a stamped, self-addressed envelope with each questionnaire.)

What should an evaluation include?

What do you want to know? Make a list of things that are important to you and important to the participant. Are those items well explained? What more needs to be said about each? Are the examples clear? Do the participants think that any of them should be excluded? Which?

Three questions are critical to most evaluations:

1. What did you find most valuable?
2. What could be improved?

Seminar Evaluation Sheet

EVALUATION SHEET

SEMINAR: _____

DATE: _____

We sincerely appreciate your reactions and comments. They help us improve by
telling us what we are doing well and what we could do better.

(1.) The **SUBJECT** was:

    ____ very well presented   comments:
    ____ well presented
    ____ so-so
    ____ not well presented
    ____ very poorly presented

(2.) What did you find most valuable?

(3.) The **SPEAKER** spoke:

    ____ excellently   comments:
    ____ very well
    ____ just well enough
    ____ below expectations
    ____ poorly

(4.) How could this seminar be improved?

(5.) The **ORGANIZATION** of this seminar is:

    ____ clear   comments:
    ____ not so clear
    ____ not clear at all

(6.) How did you hear about this seminar?

(7.) What more could we do to better meet your needs?

3. What wasn't explained but should be about this subject?

Those "most valuable" items should be kept in and strengthened: they are the heart of your presentation. Be certain they are also the core of your seminar write-up or description.

The next two must be read and evaluated closely. Some participants expect eight hours of material in four hours; others simply don't understand the subject fully and want an hour about a sub-topic scarcely worth comment. But all too often the responses zero right in on the weaknesses and soft spots, and any seminar-giver who blithely ignores this well-meant advice misses invaluable criticism.

Other questions that many want answered: Is the cost too high, about right, or too low? Was the seminar too long, the right length, or too short? What other, related subjects lend themselves to seminars you would attend? How could the speaker improved his/her presentation? And much, much more....

Is there a preferred format?

The evaluation sheet should be simple in appearance, easy to complete, printed on one side of the page only, and have ample space for replies.

You can ask the participant to fill in the seminar title and date but don't ask for his/her name or attempt in any way to identify the respondent. (Some leave a place at the end of the questionnaire for a voluntary testimonial to be used for promotional purposes. They then ask basic biographical information -- name, occupation, city/state, and age (optional), plus a signature authorizing use of the testimonial in print. Others suggest that the testimonial, with related information, be written on the back and signed.)

How should the responses to the questions be made? That depends on the kind of participants you have at your seminar. Some like to check choices; others prefer to write a word or sentence. But there's a way to cater to both tastes in most cases, as the sample evaluation on these pages shows. Except for those questions that don't lend themselves to choices, you simply follow those choices with the word "comments." It's irresistible!

Finally, are evaluations worth the time and cost? You bet. Most participants like to take part in the seminar process. They like to have a role in shaping a program to which they will send their friends. And no form of criticism will be better in quality or more directly linked to the listeners' needs than that freely offered by them. Only a fool would pass up this gift.

Chapter 20

Back-of-the-Room Sales

By simplest definition B.O.R. sales are those that come from products sold during or after seminars, speeches, or presentations. These are often displayed on a table in the back of the room, hence the term, though they can also be shown from the dias, passed hand-to-hand, or displayed in front.

They exclude workbooks, handout materials, or books and tapes included in the cost of the program. They also exclude mail order sales unless those are made and paid for at the presentation, to be mailed later.

B.O.R.'s are usually books, tapes, manuals, pamphlets, reports, newsletters, anthologies, video cassettes, and sometimes products not related to information dissemination.

How do you select and find the best products?

First you make a list of the items the participants at your seminar most need to know or have to put your message into action. If you are discussing a process and they need more detailed information about the steps required, seek a book or books with that information clearly explained. If they need examples, diagrams, blueprints, sketches, layouts, whatever, they will eagerly buy follow-up material if your seminar has ignited their interest.

You will be judged by the quality of materials offered for sale. Don't simply find something to sell to take advantage of their buying fever. The good will your seminar created will evaporate if you pass off outdated, inferior, or useless products later.

If you are explaining how to write comedy scripts, the best book on that topic should be made available, as should a book with sample scripts. You may wish to add a good book about selling scripts, another about script agenting, and still another about comedy writing in general. You note that none directly overlaps on the other. The question should be less which of two to buy but how many to buy of the complementary materials.

Let's assume that there are good books available. Evaluate what's on your library and bookstore shelves, then cross-check with **Books in Print** (both cloth and paperback) to see what is presently being sold. Read those books at hand. Ask for complimentary copies of the rest, explaining how they will be used if purchased in quantity later. Also contact the respective publishers for a commercial discount list to see how much the books will cost you in lot, whether the unsold copies can be returned for a refund, and how you establish credit. (You can find publishers' addresses in **Books in Print** or you can call 800-555-1212 to see if they have a free phone number.)

Most publishers give a 40% discount for 10 or more books ordered. You will reap about 33% on each tome, after paying shipping and suffering damage or a rare rip-off. Keep your price equal to the bookstore's list and maintain as low an inventory, until you get a feel for the sales flow, as you can and still receive your bulk discount. (It's far more pleasant and just as easy to order additional books than it is to send back crates of lost expectations.) Given a choice between paperbacks or cloth, stock up on the least expensive.

At times there are either no books to chose from or they are simply not good enough to offer for sale. That's where you should produce your own, self-publishing if the number of participants is sufficient to sell out a small printing over a two-year period or less. Read Dan Poynter's **Self-Publishing Manual** for explicit details about production and sales. Or publish through regular commercial channels.

The disadvantages of self-publishing? You must write the book, then market it! The advantage: most books are priced at eight times their actual cost, so the chance for a windfall is real -- if the book is good, has a selling cover, and is hawked with vigor. (Selling directly to seminar participants also removes the greatest expense: promotion. If the job you do during the seminar isn't promotion enough, more won't help!)

Audio-cassettes are almost always self-produced though they are seldom as lucrative, in a total income sense, as books because the demand for tapes beyond the B.O.R. scope is limited. Their production is far less expensive, inventories of 50-100 are common, and the mark-up on a 60-minute cassette, usually sold at $9.95 or higher, is seldom less than 5:1. They can also be tailor-made to your listeners' needs. And if your presentation is pleasing to hear and inspirational, tapes are a natural way to continue that intimate relationship after the formal speaking structure has ended.

Do B.O.R.'s serve any function beyond moneymaking?

You bet. With the right items for sale you can deepen and widen your effectiveness. After all, how much can you say in a few hours or a day that will remain in the participants' memories? The workbooks reinforce your main points, but any message worth hearing demands additional repetition and expansion.

They also help keep your fee competitive. If you have to include books and tapes in the seminar costs, many would not register. But by making support material optional but available, thus breaking the costs into smaller portions, many will opt to purchase the back-up items once they know why they need them and how to use them.

If the B.O.R. items are your own, are impressively packaged, contain high quality material professionally prepared, and include your name, address, and phone clearly placed, they serve as both continual reminders to those using them and valued pass-along items that will generate future consulting, booking, and business.

Can you offer the same items everywhere?

What you sell and how will depend upon the audience you are serving.

A full seminar calls for your full B.O.R. display sold after the session(s) and sometimes during breaks. Mass market audiences will prefer books, given a choice. But if you are giving a speech, the most you may be able to sell will be tape albums, which you might plug during the talk, if appropriate.

When called to talk about your new book, stage a book-signing afterward. Or at least have autographed books available for sale on the site. The least you should do is make available to all listening a copy of your mail order catalog.

What you will be able to sell should be worked out in advance with the person booking you. At universities and colleges, B.O.R. sales are understood to be part of your program so long as the sole purpose isn't to sell your goods. At seminars sponsored by businesses you won't have a display but rather will sell the items to the programmer first, to be given to the employees by the company. In other cases you must clarify first what can be sold, when, and how -- and what percentage of the take is yours.

How profitable are B.O.R.'s?

Not very at the outset, when your focus, rightly, is on the seminar or presentation. But soon enough you should shoot for a third as much in sales as you make in your fee. The rise to 50% or higher will come quickly. Beyond that it depends upon the kind of material and audience you address, how much emphasis you place on the sales, the relationship of the average unit cost and the income and need perception of your participants, and how accessible your products are elsewhere.

The single most important element in your sales, though, will be your presentation. People want to buy more good things from good people, and if your seminar or speech is indeed good, their enthusiasm will find its way into product sales.

How they are mentioned also directly affects their sale. The "hard sell" can work, of course, but every seminar-giver I know says the same thing: mention the products in passing where they meet needs. The harder you push them the more the participants resist. Just pique their curiosity, show where the items fit in, and let them sell themselves.

Do you need salespeople for your B.O.R.'s?

In small gatherings, no. But anything above about 40-50, it sure helps. That presumes you sell only after the seminar, which will lose a few sales from those who can't remain a few minutes after the final hour. If you sell during the break(s), you too need relief so you must have a helper to handle sales.

There are three sources: bring a helper along, contact the temporary worker agencies (like Manpower), or use a seminar participant and pay him/her with a product from the table. In any case the system must be simple: cash or credit cards, with the latter handled on a mail order basis where they fill in a form with their card number, expiration date, name, address, phone, and signature. They show the card with the form, they are given the products, and you clear it later by phone. You can teach this to anybody in one minute, as long as you handle the phone follow-up.

Much of the paperwork is simplified if your order form clearly lists what is available, its cost, any tax added, and the total fee. You can include this form in the workbook, as a loose page, and/or it can be prominently displayed on the table. You may also want to distribute a take-home order form that includes a fuller write-up of the products sold, the cost (including shipping), and where the order should be mailed. The take-home form can be distributed with the workbook or handed out at the door as the participants leave.

Must you have a company to sell products?

Nope. Just products. In most states you must give the governor his due, so you should find the state tax collection agency, contact it, and explain what you are doing. Be modest in your selling estimates.

Only when you wish to use a name for your company that is different than your own must you go through the fictitious business statement process. Your county clerk will explain the procedures, which are relatively simple and seldom cost more than $50. Banks will require formal notification that this has been done to open an account in a name other than your own, and the credit card accounts normally follow suit. Your income should increase considerably by making it possible to charge purchases with, at least, VISA or Mastercard.

Don't product sales damage your image?

A few people may have difficulty separating the substance of your seminar from what they perceive as "business" later on. Some people resent the collection plate in church and the artist charging for his paintings, too.

But if your presentation is honest, solid, and calls for action, and your products are precisely the same, plus they provide additional tools to make that action a reality, you should worry more that by simply ending a talk and providing nothing more you are doing a great dis-service. As long as the purchase is voluntary, you use no physical or psychological coercion, and the B.O.R.'s are clearly supplementary, the problem isn't yours.

Chapter 21

Follow-Up

Why should a single seminar terminate your contact with others eager to pay for information about a subject you know well and speak about?

True, some only want to hear what you say at your seminar. But others want to hear more. They have particular projects they want to discuss with you in detail. Or they want to bounce an idea off of you and hopefully pick up how-to tidbits in the reply. Others want you to do the work so they can get rich!

That's why a follow-up makes sense -- if you made sense (and cents) in the original presentation!

Consulting

For those who want to hire you for follow-up consultation, make that easy. Put your name, address, and phone number on the workbook and every flyer you send their way.

Don't overstate the fact that you consult during the seminar. Rather, use examples in which you solved a problem or provided a unique insight that led to success. Be sure the examples are positive! Simply say, "One of my consulting clients had a peculiar problem we might benefit from sharing..." And then omit names or telltale clues that could identify the person or firm.

Often listeners will want to discuss consulting directly after the presentation. Yet the setting is too hectic, thus inappropriate. So ask them for a business card with a number where they can be reached at, say, 10 the next morning -- or jot the number down with the person's name. Then give that person your business card, with a promise that you will call.

Others will phone you at your listed number the next day or week. If you are on the road offering seminars, make certain that the person answering those calls writes down the same information and relays it back to you the day it is received so you can respond promptly.

Products

Many in your audience will want to buy products during and after the seminar. That can be controlled with an order form available with the workbook or on the display table.

But for the many who are less impulsive (and perhaps shorter on funds) it makes sense to provide a mail order method for later purchase. Some use the same order form, simply adding the shipping costs and supplying a box for the mailing address.

A more extensive form -- let's call it a catalog -- will bring more orders. The catalog should describe in some detail every major product, in addition to its title, author, and cost. Photos of the products also increase their sale. If your catalog is sufficiently self-explanatory, many in attendance will pass it on to others who, from the descriptions, may also order your products. In fact, encourage your listeners to share them. The catalog can either be included in the workbook, with the other order form, or it can be passed out later, in each case with an explanation of how one differs from the other.

When responding to mail orders include reminder and sales material -- flyers, schedules, sample workbook pages, testimonials -- plus another catalog with the products purchased. After all, these are customers who have shown a special interest in you or your product. They are particularly likely to show further interest if you provide reasons for doing so.

Additional seminars

What drew you together in the first place was your seminar and their interest in it. The most likely field of further convergence will be related topics and more seminars, in person or on tape.

So if you will be offering other seminars about similar subjects in the near future, the participants at your first seminar should be prime recipients of any promotional material you send. You may wish to clarify in the descriptions of the other seminars how they cover new ground or explore a particular facet to far greater depth -- in other words, assure the recipients that the new seminars aren't the old seminar with just a new title or minor alterations.

If you will be offering the old seminar only, a flyer to the participants should nonetheless be sent -- if you did a good job the first time around! If the participants were favorably impressed, this gives them an opportunity to tell others about your coming program. Better yet, ask them on the flyer: IF YOU BENEFITTED FROM THIS SEMINAR, WHY NOT TELL A FRIEND?

Of course, information about the products you have for sale, plus a discreet question (Consulting? Call _____), will help pay for the promotion while it keeps your name and services before your clients.

Mailing list

A follow-up mailing to participants is possible because you had a sign-up list at or for your seminar. Those names and addresses provide the heart of your mailing list, to which you add the names and addresses of all others placing orders or making inquiries who were not in attendance. You can even break this down further by coding whether they attended the seminar, sought consulting, bought products (which in turn can be coded), inquired, and so on.

If you offer seminars or products on a continual basis, with new items added with some regularity, you may wish to send a flyer to all -- or a coded group -- at certain times of the year or when you think they would be particularly receptive. You can also rent your list to others. Contact **Standard Rate and Data Services,** 5201 Old Orchard Rd., Skokie, IL 60076, for information on how to get listed in their library "Mailing List" publications at no charge.

What do all of these categories have in common?

They will be useless as follow-up vehicles unless your seminar is good. Who wants to buy products from a person who doesn't know what he is talking about? Or sit through another seminar by a person who doesn't know how to share what he does know?

You have one chance -- one long chance. In a speech you get a few minutes. In a conversation, less. But in a seminar you are in control for hours. It's your spotlight. People pay to see you perform. So you must.

At the end of those hours the listeners must be enlightened, re-assured, in most cases inspired, in every case impressed.

Then, and only then, is follow-up worth the effort.

Bibliography

Too little of a specific, practical nature has yet been written about seminars, so if you wish to venture beyond the more general items listed below (or subsequently published) you may wish to try one of four places:

(1) reading about each component of the process (like organizing a meeting or using mail order), where there is much in print;

(2) digging through texts that mention seminars, in passing, while really discussing meetings and conferences;

(3) reading about parallel activities which have much in common with seminars, like self-publishing or selling; or

(4) keeping your eye on the **Business Periodicals Index, Education Index,** and the **SSCI** in the library for occasional articles of worth. In library listings, check seminars, meetings, conferences, workshops, and forums.

Of the current items in print directly about seminars, these are the best I could find:

How To Organize and Manage a Seminar, Sheila Murray, 1983 (Prentice-Hall, $ 6.95). The best buy around, a 204-page paperback with plenty of facts and resource guides. Weak on basic seminar development and small, one-person programs; strong on corporate, established programs. Plenty of how-to help.

How To Create and Market a Successful Seminar or Workshop, Howard Shenson, 1980 (Bermont Books, $27). Reads like a transcript of Shenson's seminar about seminars. Best if you are a professional with consulting experience. Solid, fact-filled. More for the seminar-giver headed nationally: how to program in New York, Boston, Dallas, and so on....

The Business of Seminars, Helen Myers, 1982 (Center for Seminar Management, $29.95). Quite thorough, with an abundance of booking advice (like Murray's). Closer to the beginner in tone but, in total, less comprehensive than the first two listed.

The Seminar and Conference Director's Idea Book, Anver Suleiman (Bureau of Business and Technology, $48). Suleiman offers a good, high-priced seminar about seminars, but save your money here.

The Seminar Market, Dominick Schrello, 1980 (Schrello Enterprises, $95). A lot of money for some 60 pages of text and a 63-page list of seminar providers. Some interesting data but almost nothing for the newcomer.

Speeches

MIKE FRANK, C.S.P.

Possibly no one in America is more qualified to write a book about speaking, not because he is the best speaker in America nor because he is the highest paid speaker in America, but because he has dedicated his life to every phase of the speaking business.

As a speaker, Frank has given over 2,900 speeches or workshops -- the first half without pay! The last half, over the past ten years, have seen his fees steadily rising. He has spoken in virtually every state as well as in Australia, Mexico, Malaysia, Hong Kong, the Bahamas, and the Philippines. He is a C.S.P. (Certified Speaking Professional), one of only 150 in the National Speakers Association. He offers one-hour after-dinner presentations and half-day seminars on sales, management, leadership, communication, employee relations, customer relations, and public speaking. In addition, Frank conducts sessions about the same topics of one- and two-day durations. He delivers about "fee paid" speeches or workshops per year.

As a public seminar producer, Mike Frank has coordinated, produced, and sponsored (directly or indirectly) over 150 public seminars in 35 different cities, including an annual program in Cleveland, for 16 years; one in Columbus, Ohio, for ten consecutive years; and one in Honolulu for five. These seminars feature many of the world's most prominent speakers, including Dr. Norman Vincent Peale, Paul Harvey, Dr. Robert Schuller, Bruce Jenner, Og Mandino, Johnny Bench, Bob Richards, Art Linkletter, Tom Sullivan, Zig Ziglar, Dave Yoho, Larry Wilson, Marilyn Van Derbur, Ed Foreman, Chris Hegarty, Don Hutson, and many more. Frank has featured over 70 of the world's premier speakers. Many consider him one of the most successful producers of programs of this kind.

As the owner of one of America's largest speakers bureaus, he books between 400 and 500 speeches for other speakers each year. His is the only "full-service" bureau in Ohio, yet it caters to clients throughout America and around the world. Frank is a student of professional speakers having personally previewed over 400. In addition, he has previewed over 600 audio tapes and 150 video tapes while maintaining files of 1,100 speakers.

Mike Frank was the President of the National Speakers Association in 1980 and has remained one of its most active members and supporters. He received one of the first "Distinguished Service" awards ever presented by N.S.A., and has regularly spoken at the Association's national convention, about marketing, professionalism, working with speakers bureaus, and ethics. Frank has also addressed many of the N.S.A. chapters about the same topics.

Hundreds of speakers have invested in his cassette program, "How To Market Yourself," which covers much of the material in this book. Very few have given as much time to other speakers as Mike Frank. As an advisor, confidant, and mentor to speakers, he spends 10-15 hours each week trying to help speakers with their careers. He personally answers every letter he receives from speakers. He has sent evaluations to over 300 speakers on preview tapes they have sent him. He has helped other speakers bureau owners and seminar producers -- often in competition with his own efforts. His philosophy is simple: "If I help others, it will help me in one way or another. Most importantly, I sleep well each night knowing that I provided answers for people in my business who have questions."

For further information about Mike Frank, C.S.P., please contact Speakers Unlimited, Box 27225, Columbus, Ohio 43227 (614-864-3703).

Introduction

"Selling is the highest paying hard work and the lowest paying easy work in the world," said the late J. Douglas Edwards, one of the all-time great sales trainers.

Think about that for a second. Great salespeople earn a lot of money but they also work extremely hard. At the same time there are thousands of sales people who are barely eeking out a living, most of whom are not putting in the necessary effort.

I can assure you that it's just the same in the speaking world. Thus, to paraphrase J. Douglas Edwards for the speaking fraternity, "Professional speaking can be the highest paying hard work and the lowest paying easy work in the world."

It is one of the hardest of all professions because not only must you develop yourself into a great speaker with a speech (or several speeches) to match, you must also market those skills and that material! So the purpose of my writing this half-book is to help you do both -- develop and market -- so you will be able to join, soon, the best of the professional speaking world.

Much of what I say comes from my experience working with hundreds of speakers who have "made it" and many more hundreds who have not. For the latter it is surely the most frustrating of fields. This book is written to remove those frustrations by providing solid guidance along well-tested paths. It works if you do!

Many ask why I'm willing to share so much information that will ultimately be used by others, to my financial detriment. The answer is simple. Every one of us, who are speakers, represents the speaking profession each time we go out to make a speech. If I can help other speakers grow in excellence and professionalism, it will elevate the profession for all of us.

For example, a speech you make tomorrow may reflect on me, as my speech may reflect on you. If the client you are speaking for is using a "fee paid" speaker for the first time and you do a good job, that client will be seeking many more of us for speeches in the future. Or the reverse. Equally as important is the process of marketing yourself to a meeting planner. If it is a positive and professional experience for the planner, that reflects on professional speakers as a group. If your actions are shoddy, questionable, unethical, and so on, that too will reflect on the rest of us.

That's why I want to share this information, since by helping share "how to" and ethical advice the entire speaking fraternity, as well as you and I, benefit. I want to help you grow, improve, learn, and both speak and market yourself ever more effectively and professionally.

What follows, then, are four major themes fundamental to success in speaking:

> I. Having Something To Market
> II. The Necessary Tools
> III. Your Speaking Format
> IV. Knowing How To Market Yourself

But first we should discuss a four-step guide that categorizes speakers as either amateurs or professionals, to provide you with a starting definition from which you can mark your upward progress.

Chapter 1

Amateur or Professional?

I see the speaking world as divided into four areas:

1. amateur/amateur

2. professional/amateur

3. amateur/professional

4. professional/professional

Basically defined, an "amateur" is either conceived as "one who is inexperienced" or "one who is doing something without pay." A "professional" is "one who is very skilled" or "one who does something for pay." By these definitions, then, most speakers fall into one of four combinations of these definitions.

The amateur/amateur

New speakers fit in here, those just getting started who don't expect to get paid while they learn the trade. They are new to the business. They are in their infancy as speakers regardless of the other accomplishments they've had in the past. They are still inexperienced but are willing to study, grow, observe, listen, and learn. Almost of all of us started here!

The professional/amateur

Two good examples in this category are the very experienced "Toastmaster" speaker or a similarly experienced corporate speaker. Both are professional in their skill and delivery, yet amateur because they are not nor ever have been paid to speak. Also in this group are those who conduct sessions for their company or are company spokespersons yet are not paid specifically for their speaking skills. At times you will also find professors, ministers, or lawyers who are professional/amateurs.

(This category refers less to quality of presentation than remuneration. Some of the best speakers I have heard have been at Toastmasters speech contests. In fact, a 16-year-old Korean girl recently gave one of the best professional/amateur speeches I've ever heard!)

The amateur/professional

Far too many -- hundreds, perhaps thousands -- fall into this category. They are getting paid but fall so short of professional quality they shouldn't be. A variation of this are those good enough to be paid who are receiving far more than they are worth.

Celebrities are frequently found in the overpaid group. Many receive fees in the $3000-10,000 range; some are paid as much as $20,000 for a single speech. Some are true professionals in the speaking sense. But the vast majority ride on their fame as sports personalities, authors, or stars of radio, TV, or the movies, charging outlandish fees before they hone their speaking skills.

(We recently booked a $500 speaker on the same program with a well-known news commentator who had been booked through another source for $5000. After the engagement was over, the client confided in me that the two were "not even in the same league," that the $500 speaker was ten times as good as the $5000 speaker!)

A third sub-division of amateur/professionals are those non-celebrities who are either charging fees before their skills are sufficiently developed or are charging, or raising, their rates far out of proportion to their true offering.

Again, amateur/professionals are getting paid, which makes them professionals. But they are speaking at a level far below what they are receiving, which keeps them amateurs.

The professional/professional

These are the "best of the best." They are well paid because they are consistently effective as speakers.

How do you identify professional/professionals? The National Speakers Association has bestowed two categories, the C.P.A.E. (the highest award for speaking excellence) and the C.S.P. (Certified Speaking Professional), on some 150 speakers in the entire world. All of them have delivered at least 250 "fee paid" speeches; most have given from 1000-3000.

Many of their names are famous: Dr. Norman Vincent Peale, Art Linkletter, Og Mandino, Jim Tunney, Bob Richards, and Marilyn Van Derbur.

Others aren't household names but nonetheless receive high fees because of their consistent professional excellence: Tom Hopkins, Zig Ziglar, Joel Weldon, Nido Qubein, Don Hutson, Larry Wilson, Don Beveridge, Alan Cimberg, Herb True, Danny Cox, Dave Yoho, Jeanne Robertson, Patricia Fripp, Phil Steffen, Ty Boyd, Ed Foreman, Jim Newman, Bill Gove, Ira Hayes, Art Holst, Charles Jones, Dr. Kenneth McFarland, Thom Norman, Rosita Perez, Heartsill Wilson, Sheila Murray-Bethel, Don Thoren, Robert Henry, Doc Blakely, Joe Griffith, Fred Pryor, Jim Cathcart, Somers White, Florence Littauer, and Carl Winters. The list could include at least 100 more, if space permitted.

There are other professional/professionals from outside the National Speakers Association. Paul Harvey, Barbara Jordan, John Naisbitt, Ken Blanchard, Spencer Johnson, and Art Buchwald are a few who are well known and are top speakers in every way. Their fees are quite high yet they have coupled their celebrity status with effective speaking skills to belong clearly to this category.

In addition, there are many more professional/professionals in lower fee brackets who are good enough to keep very busy. So fees **per se** don't distinguish the level of professionalism. An example might be the many who offer 80-100 speeches/workshops a year in the $300-1000 range. They are certainly no less professional than those charging far more.

How will these categories help you?

Read them closely and decide (1) where you are now and (2) where you want to be. Whether you haven't given your first speech, offer 50 a year at a fee of $500 each, deliver 75 annually at $2000 per, or are a celebrity seeking professional direction, the rest of this book is designed to help you.

And so am I. Since you have invested in this book, if you need further help just call or write anytime. You've taken the first step; the book and I will help with those who follow up. I can be reached at:

Mike Frank, C.S.P.
Box 27225
Columbus, OH 43227
(614) 864-3703

Let's get to the specifics....

Chapter 2

How To Succeed in
Professional Speaking

These are the basic steps of succeeding in professional speaking:

(1.) Have something to market. Be the best you can be in its delivery. Keep growing, learning, practicing, and developing. One of the most prominent speakers says, "Go with what brung ya." He is saying that if you have great stuff, there is no need to change its basic concept nor some of your classic stories. Many of the top speakers have used 90% of the same speech for years and it continually gets them positive results. There are some speakers who are constantly researching, updating, and expanding, which is fine. But some of the most successful have also gone too far. They have stopped using "what brung 'em" and they are not as effective nor as well received as they were years ago.

(2.) Get all the "tools" you can to be able to share with the world who you are, what you are, and how you can help the client's group. (See Chapter 4.)

(3.) Market yourself. You must find the clients. 90% of the most successful speakers realize the importance of marketing. (See Chapter 6.)

(4.) Keep working on getting better and better as a speaker.

Chapter 3

Having Something To Market

I. YOUR TOPIC

Having something to market is **the** most important element for any speaker who truly wants to become a professional in all aspects of speaking.

That is particularly important because today there are ten times the number of speakers there were just a decade ago, and with so much competition we must all be just that much better to succeed.

Yet it's not so dire as it sounds, for there are also a lot more opportunities than ever before for professional/professionals.

How do you break in and rise to the top? By having something to say -- and then honing that message, your delivery skills, and its marketing through constant attention and repeated practice.

Additional Guidelines for Speaking Success

Three elements other than solid marketing seem to be evident in those who "make it" in the speaking world -- and missing in those whose careers seemed stalled or stopped:

(1.) They speak about a subject where they have expertise, and limit the range of their speaking subjects to those and related fields.

(2.) Their topic/material is original.

(3.) They practice what they say: they are the same person off the platform as on.

Perhaps we should focus on these elements before we explore the ways that new speakers get started.

Finding a Subject

Too often I've had potential speakers ask me, "What's a hot topic today that I can get started speaking about?"

It's hard not to break out laughing because it just doesn't work that way. Professional speaking is far more than just uttering timely words. In fact very, very few speakers think of speaking as their goal early in life. Almost all get into professional speaking because they have become highly skilled in another area of life or business and they want to share that knowledge or skill with others.

Of course it is possible for someone to research a topic thoroughly, go to acting school, take in-depth speech courses, get plenty of advice, and spend hundreds of hours practicing material and become, ultimately, a professional speaker.

Yet for most, speaking emanates over the years from what they already know. They share that knowledge with others, they teach or conduct in-house sessions, they learn the communication basics over time, and then the speaking "bug" bites them. They focus on framing their ideas in a professional format, practice and practice, do further research, and market. The most important part of that process is that they begin with something valuable to say.

So if you are new to speaking and are hunting for that first topic, look to what you know that others care to hear about. Ask yourself of what you know what would others most benefit from hearing? Is it a solution to a problem? A new way of seeing their lives? Is it taking some basic truths and making them clearer and more memorable through examples, humor, juxtapositioning other truths, comparing them with historical similarities? Or is it lifting the listener from his troubles by reseeing them in a humorous vein?

Remember, for a speech to have depth and justify its being given, the speech must meet a need. What needs can you meet with a speech in a field that you already know?

Another way to find an appropriate topic is to study what other speakers are talking about, the titles they use, and the purpose of their talks, that is, the need(s) that those talks meet.

That can be done by noting the speeches reported in the newspapers, magazines, professional journals, and trade publications. Look at convention schedules, workshop offerings, extended education bulletins from nearby colleges or universities. The N.S.A. Membership Directory is an excellent source as well.

Expanding Your Topic Base

At first you will want to find one topic for which there is a listening market, develop it, and make that speech shine.

Soon enough you may want to expand your offerings, as your expertise or subsequent factual preparation warrants and your speaking skills dictate. Most move out slowly from their first topic, expanding into directly related fields, one speech at a time.

An excellent example of this is Christopher Hegarty, C.P.A.E., who was one of America's top salesmen. As you can imagine, Hegarty's initial speeches were about salesmanship. Yet as he delved more deeply into the subject and expanded his knowledge through research, interviewing, and applying new concepts, his topics expanded to include self-esteem, stress, listening, and neurolinguistics.

You don't want to have too many offerings. I have seen speakers who list 50 topics or speech titles! Versatility is fine. Most of the best speakers can relate their material and tailor their talk to a wide variety of groups, but 50 different speeches, each of substance and value?

Zig Ziglar is a classic case in point of a top speaker who sticks close to the subjects that he knows best. He speaks only about attitude/motivation, closing the sale, and religion. If you ask him to talk about telemarketing, he will direct you to someone else.

In a similar vein, the very best of the professional/professionals, like Ziglar -- Jeanne Robertson, Ira Hayes, and Jim Tunney, to mention a few -- stick to the areas of their strength. When a client asks for something else, they refer that client to another speaker or to a speakers bureau.

Keeping Your Topic or Material Original

Let's face it, there are just so many subjects that people want to hear about, that meet a need, and that lend themselves to oral presentation, so every speaker can't have singular turf on which only he or she can trod.

On the other hand, it's more than unethical, it's illegal, to take somebody else's material, lightly reword it, and claim it as your own.

Copyright for writers offers a clear guideline here. Nobody can copyright ideas. Anybody can write (or speak) about self-esteem, for example. But if somebody has written about it in a particular way, you cannot write about it the same way. In writing, the copyright is on the words in the order they are written. So you cannot use that order or you violate their rights. You must find another order -- significantly different -- for your mode of expression. The same holds true for speaking, taping, and other forms of expression.

What you must do is find either a new topic where overlapping is not a problem or a new combination of words, examples, anecdotes, and facts to convey your thoughts about a more commonly used topic.

The "key" is using real life examples to make your point. The best of the professional professionals have numerous illustrations which set them apart from others.

Giving credit to others

In a technical sense that new combination produces new material. Yet some of those components will come from other clearly identifiable sources, where credit should properly be given. Usually those are quotes or stories.

There's an adage that speakers often tell to get a laugh. It says that "the first time you use someone else's story or quote you say, 'so and so says.' The second time it is used you say, 'a friend of mine says,' and the third time it is used you say, 'as I have always said'."

I don't agree with this philosophy. I think we must give proper credit. When we state that something happened to us and in truth it happened to someone else, we are on unsound ground.

It's simple enough, really. If the material is important and you know the source, cite it. Or if you know where you heard it, give credit. There are two obvious reasons, beyond the propriety.

It doesn't hurt your standing to mention reputable sources. To mix in the company of Socrates, Abraham Lincoln, Gandhi, and Mark Twain -- to mention the kind of sources frequently used -- is good company indeed, and can't help but elevate an already solid speech.

And if you don't give credit, what does the audience think when they hear the same story, for the third time, that you are passing off as an original? You may get a laugh but the loss of credibility, just because you aren't gracious (or honest) enough to reveal its origin, isn't worth it.

For example, in 1969 I heard a story from Jesse Owens that I try to remember to give him credit for each time I use it. He may not have created it but that's where I heard it. So while I'm not saying it was original with him I feel comfortable letting the audience know that he was my source.

It's permissible to integrate good examples used by others, with discretion and proper accreditation, as long as the substance and form of the speech into which they are inserted is clearly yours. Listen to other professional speakers and learn from what they do well. The concept of O.P.E. (Other People's Experience) fits in well in the world of professional speaking. We needn't reinvent the wheel.

Let me share a story that shows how we can relate another person's story without implying that it is ours or happened to us. I first heard this from Earl Nightingale in 1966, from his famous "Strangest Secret."

The story deals with a fellow who lived at one end of a small town and worked at a factory at the other end. Every day the man walked to work. His path carried him through the downtown area past a small jewelry store. In the window of that store was a large clock. Every morning, as the man passed the jewelry store, he would stop, look at the clock, play with his watch, and walk on to work.

This went on every day for years, until one day the jewelry store owner came out and said to the man, "I apologize. I have never really taken the time to come out here and chat with you. What is it you do every morning when you stop in front of my store and then go on?"

The fellow replied, "I'm more than happy to tell you. As you may know, I am the foreman at the plant. One of my jobs down there is to pull the noon whistle at 12 on the dot. Because of that it is very important that my time be accurate, so as I stop by your store in the morning, as I have done for years, I set my watch by your clock and go on."

The jewelry store owner said, "It is a small world, isn't it? You see, for years I have been setting that big clock at 12 on the dot -- by your noon whistle!"

I think this is a great story to illustrate the potential hazards of following someone who may be following us, of following leaders rather than followers! I often embellish this slightly to tie it into the group I am addressing but I'd never claim that the story is mine.

How far must you go to extend proper credit? Perhaps the most ethical example I've heard of in the speaking business concerns a speaker who used a story often told by one of our most respected deceased speakers. It was one of those rare stories that was absolutely attributable to the man. So when it was used, the person not only gave the originator credit in the speech, he also sent his widow $1! Talk about the extra step!

Of course, personal examples are the best to use -- if in fact they happened to you or to people you know. Be sure they clearly illustrate the point you are making and that they're not made up just for that reason.

Remember, never lie to an audience, straight out or by implication. That's a lesson school teachers learn early in the game: the kids can tell. So can listeners, as much by the tone of your voice as the incredulity of the story.

Practicing what you preach

That is, off the platform be what you are, and what you claim, while you speak.

There are speakers talking about self-esteem who have extremely low self-esteem. And others talking about successful sales skills who were dismal failures as salespeople, or are terribly unprofessional in selling their services as a speaker. The danger is obvious: sooner or later the difference will catch up with them.

I know several well-known speakers who are totally different people on stage than they are off. That is okay if it is merely a matter of having higher energy level or being funnier on stage than off. But when a speaker is talking about the "power of praise," for example, throughout a speech but then gets off stage "downing" everyone he talks about or condemns someone in the audience because they weren't as respectful of him as he would like, it is time for that speaker to re-evaluate why he is speaking.

II. THE FIRST STEPS

How do you get started speaking professionally?

First you pick a topic, as we've already explained. It should be something you know well or something that you plan to research or study extensively.

Then you develop a presentation that lasts 20 to 30 minutes. With very few exceptions, new speakers begin at the "freebie" level offering speeches for no fee to civic and community groups. The time those groups usually allot to speeches is 20-30 minutes, so your initial offering is designed to fill that time slot.

Later you will want to expand that presentation to 45-60 minutes, which is by far the most sought length for a fee paid speech. Beyond that, the half-day, full-day, even two- or three-day workshops or programs constitute, in total, about 25% of the fee paid requests. Longer, in-depth sessions give you the opportunity to create more rapport with the audience. That can lead to far more cassette and book sales, if you have such items to market at your presentation.

Take the contents of that short speech, of 20-30 minutes, and outline it, using major headings, ideas, and stories or examples/anecdotes. The outline can be as detailed or as skimpy as you wish, but the presentation must be carefully planned. You must be able to read it, understand it, and practice it.

Particularly practice it. Professionals don't "wing it" on the platform. It may appear that they simply get up and speak "off the cuff." But rest assured that of every 100 great speeches you hear, 99 are well researched, developed, and practiced. It is the frequency of the repetition of the practice that creates that sense of spontaneity!

Do you think that a singer in a nightclub "wings" a song? Or a Las Vegas comedian hasn't practiced his or her material over and over? It's no different for speakers.

Even at "roasts" the "roasters" have practiced their put-downs time and again. In fact the hardest thing I ever had to do in speaking was "roast" another past President of the National Speakers Association. Mind you, that is **not** my specialty. But all the past presidents of N.S.A. had been asked to join in the "roast." I had no choice. So, despite knowing that I wasn't particularly effective doing this, I practiced my four minutes of "roasting" as much as I ever did for any speech of any length -- and still blew some of the punch lines!

Where do you practice? At home in front of the mirror. Driving to and from work. During your spare moments. In front of your spouse or another family member who is supportive of what you're doing. To a friend interested in helping you in your speaking career. **You can never practice a speech too often.** Whether it is for free or for fee, practice and practice until its delivery is flawlessly "spontaneous."

Marketing Your "Freebies"

Once you have created and learned a speech that has true value to an audience, it is time to start marketing yourself on a "freebie" basis. That "we must crawl before we walk" is also true in the speaking world. But why give it away free? Because professional speaking is more than learning a speech and saying it. It's content, presentation, pacing, projection of voice and conviction, sharing of mood and purpose ... most learned by doing. So instead of a fee you accept the opportunity to speak before a live audience and have a chance to learn the other, critical components of public speaking by doing.

It's a "win-win" situation in every way but financial. And that awaits you later, when speaking for sizable fees is the reward for those who learn the trade fully and ply it professionally.

We must "sell" ourselves to those who need speakers but don't pay fees, for they are just as concerned as fee paying clients that the speaker is good and has something to say. Not only must we convince them to hear us, their level of appreciation is usually minimal. While they need a speaker and you are doing them a favor, as well as yourself, you will get fewer kind letters and compliments than when you speak for money! Yet the free speeches are absolutely vital.

Ask any of the most successful speakers. They will tell you that they gave 50, 100, or 200 just for the pre-talk lunch or dinner before they ever got a fee.

Marketing yourself for freebies is straightforward:

(1.) Print a simple flyer outlining your background, what you have to offer, and how you can be reached.

(2.) Get or compile a list of civic and community groups who use speakers at no fee.

(3.) Mail your flyer to the program chairperson of each group.

(4.) Telephone those chairpeople after they have received the flyer.

Let's explore each of these four marketing steps.

Your "Freebie" Flyer

You can't just call a group and tell them that you have a speech to offer. Print a simple flyer which tells a little about you, your background, and your topic. A few points to consider:

(1.) The flyer doesn't have to be expensive but it must be professional in appearance.

(2.) It can be as simple and short as the example that follows. That is the first flyer I ever printed (in 1972). The one error I made in it was that it did not indicate a title or topic. However, it served as an introduction to the group to consider using me **and** as an introduction to use the day of the speech.

INTRODUCING

D. MICHAEL FRANK

Mr. Frank is the Regional Vice President for American Salesmasters, one of America's largest sales training organizations. He has addressed more than 1500 organizations throughout the United States, Canada and Australia.

Mr. Frank has worked with many of the top business leaders from all over the world while guest lecturing with his firm.

His work has brought him into contact with many of the sales training and motivational masters of our time—men such as Earl Nightingale, the late Elmer Wheeler, Dr. Norman Vincent Peale, Paul Harvey, J. Douglas Edwards, Bob Richards, Dr. Maxwell Maltz and Heartsill Wilson.

Mr. Frank, who resides in Columbus, Ohio, is a graduate of the University of Georgia with a Major in Real Estate and Insurance.

May I present to you,

Mr. D. Michael Frank

(3.) It was printed on index paper stock (about four times as heavy as regular paper). It can be any color you prefer, preferably something other than white.

(4.) A picture is not critical, but helpful.

(5.) My residence is indicated, but as you go on to a more elaborate brochure, it can be a detriment to include your hometown. (I discuss this later when talking about speakers bureaus.)

(6.) Some print their flyers on a full 8 1/2" x 11" sheet. That is fine, especially if you already have secured some testimonials you want to include on the flyer.

(7.) The example in this book was printed (in printer's language) "three up," which means that three copies come out of one 8 1/2" x 11" sheet of paper. The actual size was about 3 1/2" x 8 1/2", which was easy for me to carry in my pocket and easy for the group to work with. (Even after having sent the introduction/flyer to the group, in advance, always bring another with you the day of the speech. There is an 80% chance they will have forgotten it or lost it that day!)

Finding Those First Audiences

In (2.) we are concerned with finding eager ears to hear our gilded words. Two obvious ways to locate the civic and community groups is to ask the local Chamber of Commerce and/or the city for such a list. The third is to pluck the information from the phone book. Alas, none of these ways tells you whether they use speakers, if they pay, or what is the name of the program chairperson. That can be found out by phoning. (No one says this business is easy. You must work to give paid or free speeches!)

The groups most often found locally that do use speakers, often at no fee, are the Lions Club, Rotary, Chamber of Commerce, Sertoma, Board of Realtors, Womens Clubs, college speaking and marketing classes, and schools. Don't forget local corporations, professional or trade associations, or the P.T.A., either. If you work at it you can book 25-50 "freebies" within six months. Some speakers spend years getting through the "dues paying" part of the business. But that needn't be so. Most groups would welcome your appearance. Your job is to get good and let them know you are available and eager.

Getting Booked For No Fee

The fourth element of marketing your "freebies" talks about tenacity. Once you are certain that the flyers have been received, call the chairpeople to (a.) make sure the flyer arrived, (b.) tell why you think that audience would enjoy or benefit from hearing your speech, and (c.) ask when a decision might be expected. Not the "hard sell," but a chance for the chairperson to hear you speak, articulately and enthusiastically.

Don't just wait for them to call you. You must take the initiative. There are many well-known people in various market areas (not to mention those of us who are not well known) who would like to start their own speaking careers. Get an edge on those who, because of their egos, won't make the follow-up contacts.

Not just one call, either. Always positive, always pleasant, always speaking of benefits to the listeners, and never bragging about how great you are! As practice and persistence make good speeches, they also create platforms for speakers.

Maximizing Your Return From "Freebies"

You want to reap maximum benefits from the speech as well, in addition to what you learn while giving it and the tally in your presentation total. Three areas come to mind:

(1.) If they said, beyond the usual courtesies, that they liked what you did, and you, too, honestly agree that it was a good presentation, ask for a letter from them stating their feelings. It will be more useful if it's on the group's letterhead. Even if they sent you the regular handwritten "thank you" note, another letter in greater depth will be a valuable addition to your testimonial file. Since you spoke for no fee it's not asking too much.

(2.) Assuming, again, that you did well and were so told by the program chairperson, ask for a directory (to keep or copy) of their affiliated groups in the area -- if such a directory exists. For example, if you speak to the local Rotary Club, chances are that several more clubs exist within a 50-mile radius. If you can get a contact name for those groups, it should facilitate additional booking and thus could bring you more speaking experience soon. If there is no directory, ask the program chairperson for the names of his or her counterparts in neighboring clubs.

(3.) Study the evaluation forms you gathered from the listeners who heard you speak. This is the **only** reliable tool which truly lets you know if what you did was well received -- and why.

(4.) Record the presentation so you can learn from it later.

The last two deserve a more detailed explanation.

Evaluation Forms

Please study the sample evaluation form that follows, then return to the next paragraph so we can discuss this invaluable gauge.

Note that the evaluation form doesn't ask how the listener feels about the topic but rather how well the speaker spoke about it. Further, it breaks down that speech into its major components: opening, organization, delivery, close, etc. It offers two ways to rate the presentation, as excellent/good/fair/poor or by a 1-10 scale. The three key responses ask for the "best part of the presentation," the "least effective part," and how the speech might be improved.

Finally, the person's name and personal information is optional -- many don't ask for it at all. To further enhance the sense of anonymity (which makes the responses even more truthful) you may wish to fill in the date, company/association/group, and speaker name lines before distributing the forms.

The sample evaluation sheet may not be entirely appropriate for all forms of speeches, but there is a danger of over-adapting it to your expertise. It is better to keep it general to cover the basics of a speech. Don't feel uncomfortable about distributing these forms or putting them at the tables: it's another trade-off in place of a fee! (As I will mention later, I recommend using the form even after we are getting paid.)

I once knew a speaker who nearly exploded with energy on the platform. But his evaluation form was slanted to measure just that, and his other strengths. Naturally he looked better on the forms than he was in person. He left the business after two years, in part because he couldn't accept honest evaluations given to him in person. His evaluation forms had been misleading him all that time!

Why do I stress them so highly? Because you can't rely on the other means of measuring your effectiveness. Program chairpeople are notoriously gracious. They don't want to offend -- they just won't book you again if you aren't any good nor will they give you a good recommendation.

Evaluation Form

SPEAKER EVALUATION FORM

DATE _____

COMPANY/ASSOCIATION/GROUP_____

SPEAKER'S NAME _____

RATING OF PRESENTATION: Excellent_____   Good_____   Fair_____   Poor_____

RATING OF PRESENTATION: (circle one)
(Scale of 1 to 10 ... 10 being highest)   1   2   3   4   5   6   7   8   9   10

BEST PART OF PRESENTATION:

LEAST EFFECTIVE PART OF PRESENTATION:

Your comments about the following segments of the presentation would be much appreciated, so we can keep what works and improve what doesn't!

OPENING:

DID SPEAKER EFFECTIVELY COVER HIS/HER TOPIC (if stated):

ORGANIZATION:

DELIVERY:

GESTURES/ANIMATION:

HUMOR:

VISUAL AIDS (if used):

EYE CONTACT:

VOICE INFLECTION:

CLOSE:

OTHER COMMENTS OR SUGGESTIONS FOR IMPROVEMENT (please continue on back, if needed):

Optional:

NAME _____

ADDRESS _____

CITY/STATE/ZIP _____

PHONE __(_____)_____

Nor can you totally believe a dozen kind compliments from the audience after the speech, as welcome as they are. Because they don't tell you how the other dozen or fifty felt. But the evaluation forms will. And even if 50 of 50 give you top ratings, there are still those "least effective" and "suggestions for improvements" comments to consider while continuing to fine tune the speech.

When do you stop using evaluations? Some top professional speakers insist upon them at every session. I know several top professionals who promise the client that if the evaluations don't meet certain pre-agreed standards, they will lower their fee. In one case, the speaker doesn't charge his fee at all! That has to be the ultimate in evaluation form utilization.

Recording Your Presentation

The final way that you can reap the fullest rewards from "freebies" is to get them down on tape so you can hear what you actually said and if it came out the way you wanted it. The process is simple enough: while it is always better to have it professionally done through the sound system, you can simply place a small cassette recorder on the lectern, on the head table, or even in your rear pocket if it's connected to an inconspicuous lapel microphone.

Contrary to what you might think, a client rarely has qualms with your recording your speech.

Nor must you stop with audio-cassettes. Today, the ability to video tape yourself adds another dimension to the quest to be as good as one possibly can. Many speakers have taped several of their talks and have been shocked to see what they actually looked like and at the gestures and habits they displayed.

Almost all of the top speakers today recorded most of their "freebie" presentations so they could evaluate themselves. I know a few speakers who actually record every presentation they give and they are long past the beginning stage. It's a superb tool for self-evaluation at any stage of your development because the tapes don't lie!

III. YOUR SPEECH

It's difficult to tell you what must be in your speech for there are as many speeches as there are speakers and subjects, but let me suggest some little things that can make a difference between a good speech and a poor one.

Humor

There is an old saying in the speaking business that you only need to use humor in a presentation if you want to get paid. And while there are a handful of excellent orators who can get away without a trace of mirth, it is inadvisable to make any speech without some of it.

By no means am I suggesting that you insert jokes for the sake of a laugh, but rather you include, where appropriate, some pertinent and humorous material, usually anecdotes or observations, that is relevant to the point being made.

Let me share a story with you that I like to include in my speeches that illustrates the awareness of our children. It concerns my three-year-old son who was quite dismayed when one of our dogs died. Our other dog howled constantly at night, which become quite disturbing to the neighbors. I felt it was important to tell my son that if the howling didn't stop we might have to give the other dog away.

My son told me that he understood, but if we had to give the other dog away could we get a cat? Well, I don't like cats, yet to appease him I said "yes."

He went on to ask, "If something were to happen to the cat, could we get another dog?"

I replied, "Yes."

Then he said, "If something happened to that dog, could we get another cat?"

Again I said "Yes," though by this time I was in a quandry by his line of questioning.

His final statement was, "Dad, if something happened to that cat, I think we ought to just give up!"

The audience laughs as I did. Yet in the process we both share an insight into the awareness of children. Another "win-win" situation. By making my point with both a story and humor it will stick in the audience's memory. And later when I want to say something quite serious, the contrast will make that memorable too.

Thus if you encounter a joke, story, or anecdote with humor to share with all, see if it can be integrated into your speech to emphasize a point you wish to make. Practice it over and over so you have it word-for-word. Then listen closely to the audience's response and read to see if or how it's mentioned in the evaluations. If it gets the laugh you want, reinforces the point you wish to leave in their minds, and is positively received, great!

Avoid Offensive or Negative References

Clearly, you don't want to offend your audience, and that is particularly easy to do with misplaced or misstated humor. It's best to stay away from ethnic, religious, political, or off-color material altogether. And if something in your speech is mentioned negatively in your evaluations, it too should be expunged of the offensive references.

Do you know what the audiences found offensive in the story I just told you? After a speech in which I mentioned the incident a person told me that they were loving everything they had heard until I said "I don't like cats." Furthermore, that I might want to think about that since it was possible that 50% of the audience would tune out after that statement.

Since I was being 100% honest in sharing the story I didn't want to lose 50% of my audience by doing so! But I'll be frank with you, I used the story unchanged the next time I told it. Would you believe that another person came up afterwards and said almost the very same thing!

Well, you can rest assured I heard it loud and clear that time -- and decided that the only way I would tell the story again would be in trying to illustrate the importance of listening to comments from the audience or reading the evaluations!

Another area where offense is quickly taken is in sexual references, however innocent they are by intent. I know of another successful speaker who makes several references to women to which females in the audience respond negatively. And even though the speaker's comments themselves are not negative, the fact that references to them in the evaluations indicate displeasure, should be reason enough for that or any speaker to re-evaluate those comments.

Cussing

How do you respond to cussing? It's my guess that at least a quarter to a third of almost any audience responds negatively.

Still, I know three very successful speakers who refuse to accept that their success comes from their material and delivery rather than the extreme amount of cussing in their speeches. They don't think their success is because of the cussing, just that it adds to the presentation.

Who will tell them that an off-color story or strong language diminishes their acceptance? The meeting planner or program chairperson? Hardly ever. And if they aren't using an evaluation form, likely the laughter and applause is their only guide. Yet can a speaker remain fully effective by unknowingly -- or uncaringly -- leaving a quarter to a third of the audience uncomfortable and thus unsatisfied?

Phrases and "You" versus "We"

Three common errors distinguish the amateur as soon as he or she speaks. They are:

(1.) the flagrant overuse of "you know"

(2.) concluding a statement with "okay?" or "right?"

(3.) connecting sentences with the word "and"

Lest you think this uncommon with those presumably conscious of what they are saying, I had an occasion about four years back to preview a tape for a speaker. He was flabbergasted when I told him that I had tallied 108 times in a 50-minute presentation where he had concluded a sentence with "okay?" Today he doesn't do that twice in a speech. More recently I previewed another speaker who did precisely the same thing only worse: 116 times in 45 minutes!

Incidentally, you can see the value here of taping your presentation, as well as getting a third-person review.

I believe there is a bigger mistake that speakers, particularly beginners, make: they overuse the word "you." It makes them sound too authoritative. It sounds too much like preaching when the speaker says, "**You** should do this." "**You** need to do that.""**You** ought to pursue this."

It would be far more acceptable by an audience for a speaker to say, "**We** should do this.""**We** need to do that.""**We** ought to pursue this." It is simply much easier and more effective for you and me to talk about "us" and "we" when referring to the audience. For example, "For **us** to be successful, for **us** to be the super speakers **we** wish to be, for **us** to market ourselves the way **we** need to, **we** need to be doing this, that, and the other."

Of course you can't eliminate all references to "you." I suggest that you -- oops, we -- work on changing a reasonable percentage of them from the authoritarian "you" to the softer "we." That, for example, if "you" is used 50 times in a one-hour speech, see if that couldn't be changed to 35 "we's" and 15 "you's," or a similar shifting of pronoun choice. (The best way to do this is to listen to your recorded speech, tally the pronouns, and work on changes from there.)

The only area where the use of "we" becomes unduly confusing is when you are speaking only about yourself. Known as the "editorial I" in print, is too confusing orally. Instead of saying "We spoke in Hawaii last week and we will be speaking in Spokane tomorrow," when you really mean "I spoke...," use the first person singular when it is correct. Use the "I."

Who Can Help?

Are you afraid to speak in public? You're in the vast majority! Several major surveys confirm that the number one fear of the American public is speaking before a large group of people!

Yet you are reading this book to find out how to overcome that fear and to succeed. So if you have more hope than experience and want to test the waters before jumping in, why not join a local **Toastmasters Club**? There is usually one in any city of 75,000 or more, sometimes several. Your Chamber of Commerce can give you a name to contact. Some meet during lunch, others in the evening. Best yet, it's quite inexpensive but invaluable if you are at ground zero.

Additionally, you may want to consider a **Dale Carnegie Public Speaking Course.** These have been well received and are available in most large cities. At this writing the fees range from $400-600 for a multi-week course, and there are usually 10-40 in a class.

While the fees are considerably higher, the multi-week course usually has fewer participants and thus more individualized attention.

For even more personalized help, almost always one-on-one (and thus not inexpensive), you may wish to consult one of the following:

>Bill Gove, Florida
>Bert Decker, Northern California
>Lou Hampton, East Coast
>Bill Woodruff, Virginia
>Mike Frank, Ohio

Be sure to join the **National Speakers Association** and the local chapter if there is one in your area. You can receive specific information by contacting:

Important Information for Speakers

(1.) Photos:

To obtain reasonable prices on a quantity order of P.R. glossy photos you must send them your photo in a finished glossy state. Cost, at 8/84: 100 = $25 (4" x 5" with name on bottom)

> JEM Photo Service
> 3424 Butler St.
> Pittsburgh, PA 15201

(2.) Direct mail marketing seminar:
Rene Gnam
Box 6435-C
Clearwater, FL 33518

(3.) Meeting Planner Mailing Lists:

a. local telephone directory
b. local Chamber of Commerce list
c. state chapter of A.S.A.E. (American Society of Association Executives)

d. Corporate Meeting Planners Directory
c/o The Salesman's Guide
1140 Broadway
New York, NY 10117 $ 175   10,000 listings

e. National Association List
c/o Columbia Books
1350 New York Ave., NW #207
Washington, DC 20005 $ 350   6,000 listings

f. World Convention Dates Magazine
c/o Hendrickson Publishing
79 Washington St.
Hempstead, NY 11550 $ 60 annual subscription

g. Encyclopedia of Associations
Gale Research Co.
Book Tower
Detroit, MI 48226 $ 170

(4.) Association Membership Lists: You must be a member or buy the list.

a. American Society for Training and Development (ASTD)
b. American Society of Association Executives (ASAE)
c. Meeting Planners International (MPI)
d. National Society of Sales Training Executives (NSSTE)
e. Sales and Marketing Executives International (SMEI)
f. your state list of school superintendents

(5.) **Tape Duplicators** (for demo tapes and/or tape programs):

> National Cassette Services
> 570 Mayo Road
> Edgewater, MD 21037

(6.) **Video Tape Duplicators** (for demos or full programs)

> Telecation, Inc.
> 4770 Indianola
> Columbus, OH 43214

(7.) **Advertisements** -- some magazines where you may wish to place an ad:

> **World Convention Dates**
> **Meetings and Conventions**
> **Successful Meetings**
> **Sales Management Magazine**
> **Incentive Marketing**
> **Meeting Place**
> **Training**
> **Meeting News**

(8.) **Newsletters:**

> a. "Sharing Ideas," c/o RCBS, 18825 Hicrest Ave., Glendora, CA 91740
> b. "Speakout," official newsletter of N.S.A. For members only. NSA, 4323 N. 12th St., Suite 103, Phoenix, AZ 85014

National Speakers Association
4323 N. 12th St., Suite 103
Phoenix, AZ 85014
(602) 265-1001

The Association currently includes some 2500 members, with, in my estimation, 90% of all the professional/professionals speaking in the U.S. Similar in purpose and function to professional associations for doctors, lawyers, and realtors, an unusually high percentage of N.S.A. members actively participate and attend the annual convention and/or other available educational programs.

Space permitting, I could share scores of stories where joining the Association made a significant difference in speakers' careers, including two cases in recent years where membership led to marriage!

When to jump in full time

Not too quickly! Professional speaking is full of uncertainties even for the best and highest paid, and a good gauge of when to abandon a full-time income is when you have 40-50 engagements "on the books" at the fee you are presently quoting.

That assumes you have passed through the "freebie" stage, have been speaking on a fee paid basis, are being booked at an acceptable fee and rate, and you have 40-50 fee paid bookings in the future.

On the other hand, if you are already financially independent you can just go at it when you're ready! (For the rest of us, though, be certain you can survive a year before cutting the ties of sustenance.)

Chapter 4

The Necessary Tools

I. MARKETING TOOLS

There are as many speeches as there are speakers and topics. The difference between their being given, profitably, or not is in the marketing. So let's focus on specific marketing tools, some already mentioned in a preliminary way in the last chapter and elaborated upon here, and others now introduced for the first time.

Brochure

A good quality brochure is a critical marketing tool, though it's true that in the '60's and '70's some of the very best speakers could operate without one. With the increased competition today, however, the number of top-notch, non-celebrity speakers who make a good living without some kind of quality marketing brochure is less than five.

Brochures are more complex, more professional in content and appearance than the simple flyer used by new speakers seeking "freebie" engagements. Let's talk about their content and form here. The next chapter will tell you what to do with your brochure once you have one!)

There are so many types, styles, and concepts which can be incorporated in brochures that an entire book could be written about that subject alone. Surely a publication will appear someday that will have only samples of, say, 100 of the finest marketing brochures for speakers. (Write me if you want a few. I'll be happy to send you some samples.)

An excellent way to begin planning your brochure is to study the best brochures of other successful speakers, not to copy them but to

Patricia Fripp's Brochure: front page

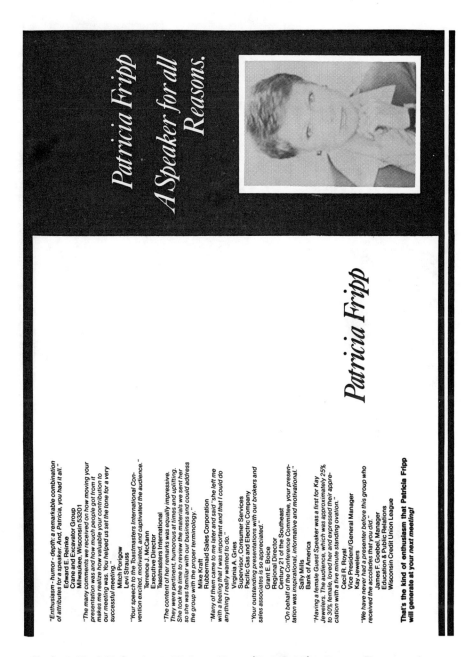

Patricia Fripp

A Speaker for all Reasons.

Patricia Fripp

"Enthusiasm - humor - depth: a remarkable combination of attributes for a speaker. And, Patricia, you had it all."
Edward E. Reinke
Crane and Excavator Group
Milwaukee, Wisconsin 53201

"The many comments we received on how moving your presentation was and how much people got from it makes me realize how valuable your contribution to our meeting was. You helped us set the tone for a very successful meeting."
Mitch Porigow
Levi Strauss

"Your speech to the Toastmasters International Convention excited, motivated, and captivated the audience."
Terrence J. McCann
Executive Director
Toastmasters International

"The content of her remarks was equally impressive. They were pertinent, humorous at times and uplifting. She took the time to review the materials we sent her so she was familiar with our business and could address the group with the proper terminology."
Mike Kraft
Rubbermaid Sales Corporation

"Many of them came to me later and said "she left me with a feeling that I was important and that I could do anything I really wanted to do.""
Virginia A. Gries
Supervisor, Consumer Services
Pacific Gas and Electric Company

"Your outstanding presentations with our brokers and sales associates is so appreciated."
Grant E. Boice
Regional Director
Century 21 of the Southeast

"On behalf of the Conference Committee, your presentation was inspirational, informative and motivational."
Sally Mills
Bank of America

"Having a female Guest Speaker was a first for Kay Jewelers. The audience, which was approximately 25% to 30% female, loved her and expressed their appreciation with a five minute standing ovation."
Cecil R. Royal
Vice President/General Manager
Kay Jewelers

"We have never had a presenter before this group who received the accolades that you did."
James F. Goebel, Manager
Education & Public Relations
Wisconsin Credit Union League

That's the kind of enthusiasm that Patricia Fripp will generate at your next meeting!

The front side of this flyer has a white base with gray (black shaded) and maroon. The gray can be seen on the right and in the photo, but the italicized type (the quotations) and the bottom horizontal stripe are also gray. The rest is maroon: the name (in the middle) and all the text on the left not in quotations. The paper is a webbed texture, three-folded, that measures 8.5" x 11".

Patricia Fripp's Brochure: back page

English accent captivates listeners from the first sentence. She talks about intriguing real-life events, delivered on the wings of humor. A log of thought-provoking substance your audience can start using *immediately.*

Patricia Fripp's participation at your next meeting, large or small, is certain to assure its complete success. She is truly a speaker for all reasons!

A Speaker for all Seasons.

Patricia Fripp makes conferences come alive, with a scintillating style that sparks the smallest breakfast session to the largest rally.

At age 14, Patricia Fripp began as an apprentice ladies' hairdresser in her native Wimborne, England. Three years later she left home to work at a French resort. There she learned that she possesses an extraordinary drive to work, learn and acquire new goals. At age 20 she arrived in America with $500 and a pair of scissors, and headed for San Francisco. Within a few years she owned her own hairstyling salon, one of the favorites in San Francisco's financial district. This exposure to exciting, creative business ideas and philosophies from some of the nation's top executives propelled her into speaking and writing. As demand for her seminar talents grew, the press began to report her phenomenal success, and in 1979, she was singly honored by election to the Board of the prestigious National Speakers Association.

Since then she has earned the designation of CSP, (Certified Speaking Professional). In 1983 she was voted by her peers to receive the CPAE award, (Continuare Professus Articulatus Excellere).

Nationally known.

Patricia is featured on films distributed by Dale Carnegie and Toastmasters International. You can hear her on a number of fine cassette programs. But best of all you can have her in person for one of her unique seminars on such topics as:

- ☒ Take Charge of Your Time
- ☒ Take Charge of Your Life
- ☒ Take Charge of Your Attitude
- ☒ A Look At Creative Thinking

...or others, all educational, fun and stimulating. Patricia delivers her talks in a free-wheeling style that captivates audiences everywhere she goes. And drives her message home!

Customized for you.

To make her message even more pertinent and valuable to your group, Patricia customizes her delivery to be most appropriate to your business activities. She prefers to move around and into the audience, and her vivacity and charming

The back side of this flyer is also gray and maroon on a white base. The maroon is limited to the top and the upper of the two bottom horizontal stripes and the following headings: "A Speaker for all Seasons,""Nationally Known," and "Customized for you." Notice the excellent mixture of photos.

glean from them the kinds of styles and concepts from which you might draw to best represent you and convey your subject.

This is another reason to attend N.S.A. conventions, workshops, and chapter meetings: to get or see copies of others' brochures. In our file of over 1100 brochures two things are evident: one, that many found guidance and inspiration in the ideas and form of others' brochures, and, two, very few of them look alike!

Some were produced by advertising agencies or graphics designers specializing in brochures, yet I feel that most speakers are quite capable of sidestepping that expense by working directly with a printer in designing a brochure that most meets their needs, if they have seen enough model brochures from other speakers to have a sense of what others are using.

Some speakers I know have paid hundreds of dollars for ideas and layouts to graphics professionals who were unfamiliar with speakers' brochures, having produced only product brochures previously. At the same time, if I were to select the top 25 speakers' brochures currently being used, 18-20 of those I'm certain were developed solely between the speaker and printer, having used others' brochures to suggest the perimeters.

The speakers using the best brochures I have seen, which would also be included among that 25, are those of Nido Qubein, Dave Yoho, Patricia Fripp, Jim Tunney, Charles Dygert, Phil Steffen, Robert Henry, Don Beveridge, Bill Gove, Heartsill Wilson, and Jim Bouton. Some of these are extremely elaborate, others are simple yet very effective.

Brochure content

When you put your brochure together consider including the following items:

(1.) a "head and shoulders" **photo**
(2.) an action **photo**
(3.) the **topics** you cover and/or your speech or workshop **titles**
(4.) five or six different **quotations** from satisfied clients. (Be sure to get their permission to use the quote from their letters. Unless you speak solely to a limited number of industries or locales, seek as wide a spread of your sources as possible. For example, a speaker recently printed a beautiful brochure that included five glowing testimonials. The problem was that four of those five were from insurance clients, which would imply to those receiving the brochure that the insurance business was his prime clientele. In actuality, insurance only represented about 30% of his business.

When brought to his attention, he reprinted the next time with quotes from five different industries and associations!

(5.) **quotes from the speaker:** quotes, concepts, ideas, or humor in your own words

(6.) **N.S.A. logo,** if you are a member

(7.) indication that you are a **C.S.P.** or **C.P.A.E.,** if you are

(8.) your **credentials** and/or **background**

(9.) a **sample list** of some of the clients you have spoken for, other than those included in the testimonials

(10.) what **distinguishes** you from other speakers

(11.) **quotes** from other speakers

At the same time, exclude one item: your **fees.** Some speakers make no mention of fees at all. Some indicate "provided upon request," which allows them to study the situation in depth to see how it fits into their fee schedule (or whether it is a rare negotiated exception). And others include a "fee range" on their brochure.

The "fee range" might state: "Fees range from $1000-2000, based on location and length of presentation." This has the benefit of telling the potential client your "ballpark" charge rate. In many cases it will get them to call you. In others, if all they can afford is $400, it saves you from having to turn them down.

Brochures and speakers bureaus

If you plan to work with speakers bureaus, now or in the future, put your address and phone number in one place **only** on the brochure, preferably on the front or back instead of the inside pages. **Keep it confined to a space 1" high by 2 1/2" wide, maximum, so the bureau can place its label over it.** If you list your name and address several times or in huge print it is impossible for the bureau to cover it without destroying the looks of your brochure.

Why not ask your printer simply to leave your name and address off of either 10% of the printing or 300 copies? It only costs a few more dollars and lets you use the name/address size you wish on the rest. Should you wind up with a few of these for your own use, cover the open spot with your own label!

Also leave off of your brochures the name of your home town as well as where you work or teach, if either of the latter is applicable. Contrary to what you may think, not one of a hundred planners cares about that information. But bureaus care a great deal. They know that however strong a rapport they build with clients some will try to work around them. If your brochure even hints at where you work or live, many will try to contact you directly. You might get the speech, but if the bureau finds out, you will probably lose the opportunity of working with them in the future!

Mike Frank's Brochure: front page

MIKE FRANK C.S.P.

PROFESSIONAL SPEAKER, TRAINER, AND CONSULTANT

ONE OF AMERICA'S MOST DYNAMIC SPEAKERS

HERE'S WHAT A FEW OF MIKE'S CLIENTS SAY ABOUT HIS APPEARANCES:

"Your presentation on creative salesmanship and motivation was second to none." .... **Dennis Gougion, S.M.E.—CENTRAL IOWA**

"Our people were quite excited about your talk. I'm pleased to say they are already using many of your ideas." **Ken Rubin, Regional Manager—CASUAL CORNER**

"Mike has addressed our salespeople four times. He has more to say, humorously and educationally, than most 'Big Name' speakers. .... **Norm Cheezrown, CHESROWN OLDSMOBILE**

"The reports on your program were absolutely fantastic. Our people are still raving about your presentation." .... **Jim Goebel, WISCONSIN CREDIT UNION LEAGUE**

"The Critique Sheets show you received an A + Rating and you were the highest rated speaker of the five professional speakers on the program." .... **Anyan Gordon, U. of Alabama (In conjunction with ALABAMA ASSOCIATION of REALTORS)**

"Thanks again for an idea-packed, information jammed, stimulating session. You were again a star performer, but knew you would be beforehand." .... **John Kolar, AMERICAN DIE CASTING INSTITUTE**

WRITE or CALL:

D. MICHAEL "MIKE" FRANK, C.S.P.
P.O. BOX 27225
COLUMBUS, OHIO 43227
(614) 864-3703

SOME OF THE 2,800 GROUPS MR. FRANK HAS ADDRESSED:

C. E. Glass (Combustion Engineering)
International Alloy
Dale Carnegie
Burroughs
IBM
NCR
Xerox
Master Marketing Corp.
Sales Training Institute
West Bend
Copco Paper
N.A.S.E.
Levitz Furniture
Du Bois Chemical
Ohio Harvestore
Marks Tractor
Sigma Phi Epsilon Fraternity
Pi Sigma Epsilon Fraternity
Clark Equipment

Hundreds of Retailers

Hundreds of Direct Sales Companies

Hundreds of Real Estate Firms

Hundreds of Insurance Companies and Agencies

Hundreds of Investment Companies

Hundreds of Automobile, Truck & R.V. Dealerships

Hundreds of Industrial Sales Firms

College, High School, and Junior Achievement Groups

NUMEROUS:
S.M.E. Meetings
Real Estate Boards
Insurance Associations
Employment Agencies
Radio and TV Stations
Land Companies
Miscellaneous Associations
Health Spa's
Banks, Savings & Loan Groups
Credit Union Leagues

This flyer is three shades of blue, plus one black/white photo (under the words MIKE FRANK) on the front. The background is light blue. A medium blue is used for the background for the panels that begin "Some of the 2,800 groups..." (on the front) and "Comments" (on the back) as well as the words MIKE FRANK on the front and both photos on the back. The rest is printed in dark blue. The paper is a heavier rag texture, and the measurements are 8.5" tall by 11" wide, folded into the panels.

Mike Frank's Brochure: back page

HONORARIUM:

SPEAKING AND CONSULTING FEES RANGE FROM $600 - $1,500 ... BASED ON LOCATION AND AMOUNT OF TIME INVOLVED.

ALL FEES QUOTED ARE PLUS EXPENSES
(COACH AIRFARE • PRORATED WHEN POSSIBLE)

MEMBER NATIONAL SPEAKERS ASSOCIATION

COMMENTS

MIKE, LIKE MOST OTHER PROFESSIONAL SPEAKERS, HAS DOZENS OF TESTIMONIAL LETTERS FROM GROUPS HE HAS ADDRESSED. THE REAL TEST, THOUGH, IS WHAT OTHER SPEAKERS SAY:

"Mike is one of the best young speakers, trainers, and businessmen in America today" ....
Bob Richards, Olympic champion and speaker

"Mike Frank has the rare quality of being able to transfer feeling as well as thoughts, because he has lived the principles he expounds. He is one of the few speakers I would recommend without reservation ....
Cavett Robert, C.P.A.E.

"Serious, dedicated, enthusiastic men are hard to come by. Mike has done the job in the field and does it professionally from the platform. I like Mike and yoursulf, too." .... **Ira Hayes, C.P.A.E.**

"It's hard to pinpoint what makes an artist, but you have that elusive quality as a speaker. You are a real professional" .... **Ed McFaul**

"Mike, we keep hearing raves about your presentations at our Pi Sigma Epsilon meetings. Thanks for doing a super job for us, twice" .... **Don Hutson, C.P.A.E.** (1976 National President of National Speakers Association and Pi Sigma Epsilon Business Fraternity)

****

HE CAN EFFECTIVELY SPEAK ON:
CREATIVE SALESMANSHIP (1-5 Hours)
MOTIVATION (1-3 Hours)
MANAGEMENT (1-5 Hours)
RECRUITING (1-5 Hours)
COMMUNICATION (1-3 Hours)
LEADERSHIP (1-3 Hours)
CUSTOMER RELATIONS (1-3 Hours)
EMPLOYEE RELATIONS (1-3 Hours)
TIME MANAGEMENT (1-4 Hours)
TERRITORY MANAGEMENT (1-3 Hours)

ADDITIONAL SERVICES AVAILABLE:
• Films and video tapes of top speakers
• Audio cassettes of top speakers
• Public seminars with top speakers
• Consulting

CREDENTIALS

• BBA - UNIVERSITY OF GEORGIA
  (MAJOR - INSURANCE/REAL ESTATE)

• WORKED HIS WAY UP FROM SALESMAN, TO MANAGER, TO DISTRICT MANAGER, TO REGIONAL MANAGER, TO NATIONAL SALES MANAGER, TO VICE PRESIDENT OF SALES OF A MAJOR U.S. CORPORATION .... WITHIN 4 YEARS AND BEFORE HE WAS 28 YEARS OLD.

• HAS SPOKEN TO OVER 2,800 AUDIENCES IN THE UNITED STATES, CANADA, AUSTRALIA AND MEXICO ... MORE THAN MOST SPEAKERS ADDRESS IN A LIFETIME.

• CONTRIBUTING AUTHOR IN RECENT BOOK, "STAND UP, SPEAK OUT AND WIN"

• HE IS IN FINAL STAGES OF HIS SOON TO BE RELEASED BOOK, "REALISTIC THINKING AND POSITIVE DOING."

• HE IS ONE OF THE YOUNGEST SPEAKERS ON THE MAJOR SPEAKING CIRCUIT IN NORTH AMERICA. IN ADDITION TO OWNING ONE OF THE MIDWEST'S LARGEST TRAINING AND CONSULTING FIRMS AND SPEAKERS BUREAUS.

• HE WAS THE 1980-81 PRESIDENT OF THE PRESTIGIOUS, NATIONAL SPEAKERS ASSOCIATION.

• HE HAS MADE OVER 19,000 "COLD-CALL" FIELD SALES PRESENTATIONS

• HE HAS "FIELD TRAINED" OVER 300 SALESPEOPLE IN 10 DIFFERENT INDUSTRIES

• HE IS A G.R.I. INSTRUCTOR

• HE IS ONE OF ONLY 95 SPEAKERS IN THE WORLD TO RECEIVE HIS PROFESSIONAL DESIGNATION (C.S.P.) FROM THE NATIONAL SPEAKERS ASSOCIATION.

• HAS SPOKEN ON PROGRAMS WITH:
  DR. NORMAN VINCENT PEALE   IRA HAYES
  DR. ROBERT SCHULLER   ZIG ZIGLAR
  EARL NIGHTINGALE   JESSE OWENS
  ART LINKLETTER   BRUCE JENNER
  BOB RICHARDS   WOODY HAYES
  PAUL HARVEY   CAVETT ROBERT
  OG MANDINO   DR. WAYNE DYER
  JERRY LUCAS   J. DOUGLAS EDWARDS
  AND MANY MORE

• HE IS LISTED WITH:
  SUCCESS LEADERS SPEAKERS SERVICE
  DARTNELL SPEAKERS BUREAU
  SPEAKERS UNLIMITED .... S.M.E.I.

While that sounds okay to you, it was the bureau that sent your information to them. It took the time and money to get them to respond. So that bureau deserves to have the booking and get the commission.

Brochure size

How you will use this brochure will largely determine its size, which in turn will directly affect its cost.

If you plan to mass mail your brochures the most economical size should be foldable or insertable into a #10 regular business envelope. I have seen brochures as large as 11" x 22" and as small as 6" x 8 1/2" inserted into that holder, but most are three-fold items that open to 8 1/2" x 11".

You can normally fit most of what is needed on an 8 1/2" x 11" brochure. But you needn't be limited artistically to that size. Brochures are a way to show your creativity to clients. If you go larger, think of having your brochure insertable into a 9" x 12" envelope. Oversized or custom-made odd-sized envelopes can get very expensive, though they do get noticed if for no other reason than their uniqueness.

Quantity and cost

I have seen very effective brochures printed in reasonable quantities that cost the speaker as little as $400. I've also seen brochures that cost more than $10,000. Work within your budget and artistic and speaking capabilities.

Unless you have a large mailing planned, keep your first printing to 1,000-5,000. No doubt there will be minor changes you will want to make after the first and second printing before you will be 100% satisfied. Also, updated testimonials, photos, and speech titles will require reprinting on a regular basis.

Be sure that more than you and the printer proofread the brochure! (If you find errors after it is printed, the printer will remind you that he prints, you proofread!) The more who read it first, once it is ready to set in final form, the better. You will be too close to it to pick up the errors that an educated, impartial reader will spot instantly.

My guess is that only 10% of the brochures ever get printed without some error. Among my brochures -- for my speeches, our public seminars, and the bureau -- I have printed over 100 different brochures during the past 14 years. To my embarrassment, after five or six readings of each we usually still find errors! So you can't afford to be too careful with proofreading.

A close friend, after six proofings, had a seminar brochure printed. It nonetheless included the price he had charged for six years instead of a new, higher price. He had to reprint -- a $2,000 lesson!

I make the following offer to you, free, as I have to dozens of other speakers: if you will send me your planned marketing brochure after it is typeset but before it is printed I will gladly proofread it and offer any suggestions I can. But **before** you print! (It's far less costly to make changes after typesetting and before the "plate" is made, than afterwards! And once the error is in print....)

Final brochure thoughts

One, when you are planning your first brochure you might consider coordinating in color, typestyle, paper stock, and ink all of your printed items: brochures, stationery, envelopes, business cards, and "thank you" or note cards.

Two, even those speakers who now have the very best brochures in the industry didn't start that way. They began with something far more modest, then worked up in form and cost as they became more successful. Like you and your speaking, your brochures will improve with close attention, experimentation, and growth.

Brochure mailing: bulk versus regular postage

If you send a few letters, they must go first class, which costs 20 cents as this book is published. But if you send 200 or more like items, you can get a bulk rate permit from the post office for $40 and send them for 11 cents each!

Most of us should use the bulk rate for mass mailings. But let me suggest that you forgo the common pre-imprinted mailing indicia, or bulk mail box in the upper right-hand corner on the envelope. Be sure your envelope or mailing piece is creative. No mailing should go out looking like a bulk rate circular, either from its looks or type of postage. Instead, buy 11-cent precancelled bulk rate postage stamps. These look like regular first-class stamps -- particularly the new series of mail carriers, the motorcycle, the old-time mail wagon, etc.

It takes willing helpers: you, the spouse, and kids! My wife and I have licked about half a million stamps in the last five years, usually watching TV late at night! The end result is a mailing piece that looks first class, gets more attention, and costs 9 cents less!

I'm not against first-class postage. But when you do use it, buy commemorative stamps. They draw more attention, are far more attractive, and are better received than those on the roll or off the meter strip.

Brochure mass mailings

We just showed you how to save 9 cents per mailing, but don't be deceived: it can be plenty expensive nonetheless.

If we send out 10,000 brochures tomorrow and expect to get 100 speeches from them, we are kidding ourselves. One thing is certain: 10,000 more people will know about us, even though 6,000 threw the brochure away without looking at any more than the name. That means 4,000 did something with it: opened it, looked at it, maybe read it. But only 1,000 kept it. And if we get two speeches from that thousand, we're lucky.

This is not to discourage you. It's to help you evaluate mass mailings realistically before mortgaging the house to get your brochure in circulation.

Overstatements

How often have you heard someone referred to as "the world's greatest _____" or "America's number one _____" with nothing more to substantiate it than the statement itself?

Speakers are prone to doing this, and I think its effect is far more negative than positive. They include such overstatements in their introductions; their brochures are rent with similar exaggerations. While listeners and meeting planners smile and shake their heads. Most people just aren't that naive!

Of course, some are told that they are the best motivational speakers in the country or the best sales trainers in the world or that they own the best speakers bureau in existence. And it could be so: somebody is or owns the best. But proving it would be next to impossible.

So why not say "one of the ...."?

Or get such praise in writing, in a testimonial letter, and quote that letter in the brochure, with the source of such good news clearly attached. Enough such letters in that brochure from people who should know and its readers will get the idea, modestly proposed, without being turned off by the undocumented headline, "The Best Speaker In The World, Now or Ever!"

Two examples more than prove the point. I once knew a speaker who printed in his prepared introduction that he would be receiving the

C.S.P. the following July -- before he even applied! As it turned out, his application was rejected. Or can you picture a girl who has just won her city beauty pageant allowing herself to be introduced in the following months as the person who is soon to be crowned Miss America? Is this really much different?

Demonstration Cassette Tapes

Quite simply, you will lose business if you don't send a solid demo or preview tape when a client requests one.

Many feel that they speak or sound far better in person than on tape -- sometimes incorrectly. Thus they are seldom happy with their demo/preview tapes. And because they don't like what they hear, they either don't have them made or don't send them out.

Yet there are clients who require a demo tape before hiring a speaker, and I know I have lost engagements because I didn't have one at the time it was requested. I've also lost engagements because the demo tape was not as good as it could have been.

So let's discuss, in seven steps, what goes into producing a good demo cassette now, then how they are used in the next chapter.

(1.) Record one of your 30- to 90-minute presentations "live" at a meeting that has a good-sized audience of at least 100, preferably 200 or more. Be sure it is recorded professionally through the sound system. If you have more than one presentation, you take your original material in a different direction, or you employ some completely different material based on different types of audiences, then you may want to record two or more presentations.

(2.) If the presentation wasn't recorded on a cassette, get the recording company to give you a copy of it in that form. Listen to it to see if you were "on," if the audience was receptive, and if it is a fair representation of how you sound and what you say. (If you're not sure, ask a "mentor" or a friend who has heard you speak.) If it isn't a good tape, record again at another presentation, until you are satisfied with the original "rough" copy. Remember, by editing you will be able to "clean up" some of the rough edges.

(3.) Go to the studio to edit the tape with a technician, to get rid of the unneeded fluff words, stutters, mistakes, or whatever else you feel should be deleted. It can take many hours to edit a demo to your satisfaction, and it can cost you $100-300 just for the editing, unless you have a good tie-in with a professional-level technical editor or you can work out some kind of trade. When you are done you may have eliminated anywhere from 2 to 20 minutes!

(4.) You must now decide whether you want some "gingerbread" added. That means

    (a.) studio-recorded inserts of explanations before, during, and/or at the end of the tape

    (b.) special music inserted at the beginning, the end, and/or at key "bridge" areas in between

    (c.) 1- to 3-minute excerpts of your talk or talks. (Some clients and bureaus prefer the whole talk while others prefer 20-25 minutes of excerpts. I prefer the whole tape, but to cover all bases you can do one of each, leave the whole edited talk intact as well as make a demo of excerpts. If you do a tape of excerpts, though, make sure that at least some of those excerpts contain material of value. I've heard some demos that didn't have enough solid content to enable the meeting planner to understand what that person really did or spoke about.)

    (d.) inserted testimonials from some of your clients at the beginning, the end, or on the flip side.

(5.) Don't close your tape by giving your address or phone number -- nor should that be included elsewhere in the recorded message. The best way to convey this information is to have a studio voice inserted at the end of the tape saying, "For further information on how to schedule (John Doe) to speak, please contact us at the address or phone on the label on this tape."

One problem this averts is the speakers bureau's concern of the client contacting you directly. If you state your address or phone, they must edit it out -- an unnecessary expense of time and labor. Another problem is if you move or change phone numbers but the previous numbers remain on the cassettes in circulation or use. By directing attention to the label, you can update your labels as necessary while the speakers bureaus can just apply their labels to your demos.

(6.) Get advice from speakers or speakers bureaus you respect about your finished product. Speakers bureaus, in particular, deal constantly with meeting planners, so their input is likely to be direct, honest, and based on current needs and practices.

Once again, let me make this book pay off for you several times over: I'll gladly evaluate your demo tape if you'll send it to me and give me 10-14 days to get it back to you. Even if it's of lesser quality, to help you get a feel for what should go in the final product. No charge!

(7.) Once you are sure that your tape is as good as possible, have it duplicated in a quantity sufficient to last for months. I'd suggest having 50-100 made since the cost of duplicating is quite low compared to the cost of recording and editing. With care you can get the duplicating in that quantity, with labels, for as little as $1 to $1.50 each.

Some buy their own duplicating machines. They are available for as little as $200, which duplicate one tape at a time. Others cost as much as $3000, which duplicate many at once and much faster than their smaller counterparts. If you live where it takes a long time to get duplicated tapes produced, you might consider buying a duplicator.

Video demomonstration tapes

These are becoming more important. In our bureau we must send audio preview tapes to about 50% of our client inquiries. We are now having to send video preview tapes to about 30%, and that percentage is increasing. So you may want to strongly consider the time, effort, and cost necessary to produce such a video demo.

The procedures vary little from the audio cassettes, with the major difference being the length. It is best for the finished product to be 15-20 minutes long. Thus the presentation you tape will either have to be a very short talk or you must produce an excerpt tape, with bits and pieces from a longer presentation.

Editing costs on video are even higher than on audio, so if you are reducing a 90-minute program into a 15-minute tape, it will cost plenty in time and money, unless you can trade this time with a video company, a client who has video-editing capabilities, or a TV station.

I mentioned trading services for tape editing earlier. Consider it seriously, for these and other services or expenses. You have a tradable commodity, your speaking or consulting talents for their organization, in full or partial exchange for your service needs. Or use the skills about which you talk as the core of the swap.

Handle your name and address on your video demo as we suggested in (5.) above, except that here you both ask and have it appear on the video screen that they should contact you at the address and phone that appears on the tape label.

For some reason, many speakers like their video demos more than their audio tapes. (After 18 years in the business I'm still not completely satisfied with either of mine. You just have to keep working on them, often retaping time and again.) I've found that if clients don't respond favorably to your video tape, if it's good and shows you at your best, you probably won't want to speak to their group. That is, they're probably not going to be pleased even if they do book you. In those cases it's probably better to refer them to another speaker or to a speakers bureau to solve their needs.

Finally, if you send a second class production to a meeting planner, that will make a negative impression on him or her. If you're going
to send a demo, it should be the best -- in audio or video -- that you
can produce. Demo tapes are tools to sell you and your services. Poor
tools don't make good sales.

Testimonial Letters

Positive letters from satisfied clients always have been and
always will be strong marketing tools. Yet there are many speakers who
throw them away, file them out of sight, or make a few copies but
never aggressively use them.

So let's focus on how to get the testimonial letters and what, in
general, to do with them now. We'll be even more specific on their use
in the next chapter.

The first thing to do with a strong, positive letter when it arrives
is to take it to your local quick printer and have 100 clear copies made.
(Do the same with the other testimonial letters hiding in your file.) Use
the variety of colors the printer has on hand: pink, canary, light blue
and green, ivory, goldenrod, buff, etc. Print each letter on one color
only so they won't look alike when you send them to the same client.

Devise a filing or cubbyhole system so you can easily find the
letters when you need them. After you accumulate a sizable collection,
you will be able to respond to the specific type of industry that is
seeking information or that you are approaching. Thus when I get an
inquiry from an insurance company, I pull out four or five letters from
previous insurance clients, knowing that there will be a rainbow assortment of particular interest to that group. Remember, the testimonials
only help when we get them in the prospects' hands.

I recently spoke in Florida because of a testimonial letter I had
sent. The letter cited a comment I had made at an earlier meeting, and
the general manager at the Florida firm said that that comment was
what sold him on me. Every active speaker using testimonial letters can
give you a dozen similar examples.

To reduce the sheer volume of paper being mailed, when you have
four or more positive letters from the same industry you may wish to
reduce each and combine them on the same page. You can even have
four or so printed on the back! That's both cost effective and impressive.

In the past year I've had some good speakers tell me that they
weren't getting as many testimonial letters as they used to. There are
two likely causes: either the speaker isn't as good now as when the

letters were flowing in or the meeting planner isn't taking the time to write the letter.

Being the best speaker that you can is what this book is about, and will, hopefully, help in the first case.

But when the lack of a letter comes from lassitude on the part of the letter writer, jar that letter loose by asking for it! The procedure is simple and is never demeaning, since you only ask when you feel you did a good job and/or when the meeting planner tells you that he was extremely pleased.

There are three times when you can most comfortably request the letter:

(1.) before you leave the speaking site
(2.) when you send your invoice for the fee and expenses
(3.) after you have received payment for the invoice but no letter was sent voluntarily

In the first case, after they have either told you or implied that you were well received, all you need do is get them to reconfirm that verbally and ask if they would be kind enough to share that input -- whatever they said or they want to say -- in a letter under one of their letterheads. You'll find that 80% say they will and about half actually follow through.

Some speakers have 500 great letters in their files while others have 1,000. The latter simply weren't afraid to ask the meeting planner to do something they were pleased to do. Others simply don't take the time to ask!

Public Relations Jackets

These are used by many of the most successful speakers and, while costly, are effective. They are usually 9" x 12" envelope-like holders sent to clients when they request support material. In them you can send your brochure, testimonial letters, a demo tape, your introduction, a photograph, etc. The appearance is far more professional than simply dumping a handful of items into an envelope. While you may not have seen them for speakers, many companies use them to send multiple pieces of literature about the company or its products.

Handouts

I have assorted thoughts about this topic, for there is no **one** way to cover the handouts needed for the full range of speaking. For speeches there may be no handout at all. For seminars, you may distribute reams of pages artfully bound. Plus many varieties in between.

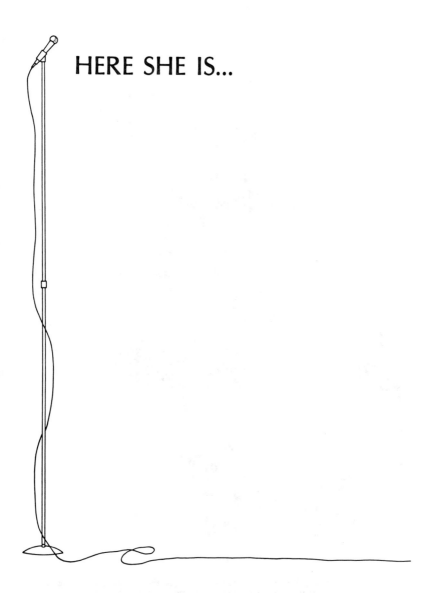

HERE SHE IS...

This simple P.R. jacket is made of textured white paper, with the microphone in black and the words "HERE SHE IS..." in bright red. On the left inside flap, of white, is the name "Jeanne Robertson," in the same bright red. That's it. The jacket measures 9" wide by 12 1/8" high; it is rounded on the upper right corner. The flaps are 4" high inside, open in the center and bound on the outsides. Nothing on the back.

The front of Patricia Fripp's P.R. jacket is four–colored. The background is white on a glossy paper stock. The photo is black. Both of the "G's" have bright red in the center, with the larger "G" a shot of red that emerges from the photo and ends in an arrow. The rest is dark blue, including the border of the "G's." The back of this jacket has three b/w photos of Patricia speaking, plus a blue N.S.A. emblem, while the center flaps, 4.5" high, include a b/w photo and, on the left, biographical information about the speaker (in blue), and on the right, also in blue, comments from the presentations given. The jacket measures 11 5/8" high by 9".

SPEAKERS UNLIMITED

"OUR ONLY BUSINESS SINCE 1966 HAS BEEN
SPEAKERS AND THEIR SERVICES"

- **SPEAKER'S BUREAU**
- **PUBLIC SEMINARS**
- **16 mm FILMS**
- **VIDEO TAPES**
- **AUDIO TAPES**
- **CONSULTING FOR:**
  Business, Sales, Management,
  Personal and Meeting Planning

SPEAKERS UNLIMITED
BOX 27225
COLUMBUS, OHIO 43227
(614) 864-3703

This jacket is dark blue with reversed (white) printing. The words "Speakers Unlimited" in the white box are gray. It has a glossy texture on the outside. The inside flaps, also glossy, are 3.5" tall and blue with a gray "Speakers Unlimited" printed on each flap. The right flap has incisions, near the center, to hold a business card. The jacket measures 11 7/8" tall by 9" wide.

Mike Frank's P.R. Jacket: back

SPEAKERS UNLIMITED

"ONE OF AMERICA'S LARGEST SPEAKER'S BUREAUS"

"OHIO'S ONLY FULL-SERVICE SPEAKER'S BUREAU"

TOPICS/TYPES OF SPEAKERS

- ✢ Athletes
- ✢ Authors
- ✢ Celebrities
- ✢ Communication
- ✢ Customer Relations
- ✢ Employee Relations
- ✢ Exercise
- ✢ Humorists
- ✢ Leadership
- ✢ Magicians
- ✢ Management
- ✢ Memory Training
- ✢ Motivation/Attitude
- ✢ Nutrition
- ✢ Personal Development
- ✢ Recruiting
- ✢ Sales
- ✢ Self-esteem
- ✢ Stress Management
- ✢ Territory Management
- ✢ Time Management

TYPES OF EVENTS

- ✢ Banquets
- ✢ Conventions
- ✢ In-service Programs
- ✢ Keynote
- ✢ Luncheons
- ✢ Rallies
- ✢ Sales Meetings
- ✢ Seminars
- ✢ Spouse Programs
- ✢ Workshops

SPEAKERS UNLIMITED
BOX 27225
COLUMBUS, OHIO 43227
(614) 864-3703

Some speakers like to give out workbooks that contain all the material they will say, to be followed item by item as the program unfolds. Unfortunately, many attendees will read ahead. Others will wonder why they needed to hear the speaker if the contents are all in print.

Others like to hand things out page by page. Which is easy to do with a small, close-sitting group. But get deep into double digits in attendance and it becomes very hard, and at three or four digits, impossible.

Whether in a packet or given out by the page, I feel strongly that the material should not exceed by much what is said. If you distribute ten times the material that one could possibly cover, your audience will feel cheated -- there was so much they never heard! You could explain precisely what will be covered and explain the rest as follow-up support material, but that's risky. And if you skip around, ending with wishful "maybe we'll get to the rest the next time!", guess who won't be speaking the next time!

If you send an outline of the material you will cover to a public seminar sponsor, cover it! I've had speakers send outlines and only talk about a portion of them. The result is predictable: unhappy clients! We promote the speaker and what he or she will say based on that outline. So everybody looks foolish when it's not followed A to Z.

Who pays for handout materials? That must be negotiated in advance, unless the cost is insignificant and you want to pick up the tab. Speakers assume that the client must pay this cost. But the client must pay only for what has been mutually agreed upon. So if you wish to add 50 cents or $5 per person for handouts, include that in the agreement. But if it's a pittance, pay it yourself.

Some speakers use a "profile" or extensive workbook which may cost them, say, $2 to buy or print. Obviously, in this case, the client should told of the cost in advance. Some speakers will charge the client a fair fee, plus $2 per person, to cover their cost of the workbook. Other speakers might charge $5 per person for the workbook, to build in some profit. That's okay. However, I know some speakers who would charge $15 per person! I feel it is unfair and unprofessional to demand that much profit if they have also charged a fair speaking fee.

Books and Cassette Programs

These help speakers in two ways. They are excellent marketing tools. Many speakers will send some or a complete sample of their products to meeting planners or speakers bureaus to help secure an engagement. Books and cassettes -- well packaged and professional in topic and development -- are powerful tools in demonstrating one's grasp of and position in their field.

They are also money-makers. A few top speakers earn in excess of a million dollars a year from tape or book sales. Many more can match or top their speaking fees through product sales, made either to the attendees (usually at public seminars) or directly to clients for their distribution.

One of the most important steps that speakers must take is to secure the client's or bureau's permission, in advance, before selling products at a presentation.

Rather than confronting the meeting planner two minutes before speaking to ask for permission to sell books or tapes, have this request discussed and approved at the booking stage. And you must adhere to your promises. If you say that you will discuss the items (a "selling commercial") for a maximum of four minutes, then four minutes (or less) is what you must take.

Likewise, if you book through a bureau and tell them that your "commercial" will last four minutes, the bureau will make that promise to the planner. But if you actually talk 20 minutes about your products, the bureau will get "burned," you most likely won't be booked by it again, and any positive testimonial letter will be lost.

So if you sell books and tapes, make it part of your negotiations, be honest, and then adhere to your promises.

Designation

If you are a C.S.P. or a C.P.A.E., use it. Some who are distinguished by these designations don't, no doubt because the designations are still new. But so were other designations of distinction, like the C.P.A. and the C.L.U. (in the insurance business). The C.S.P. and C.P.A.E. will take hold, as the others did. So it should be worked into your printed material and introduction -- after you've earned it!

Presentation Taping by the Client

Many times having a client professionally tape your presentation can be a big marketing plus for you. But it should be arranged in the initial negotiations and you must know why the taping is taking place, so that you can wisely respond as to whether you grant permission.

Alas, too often the meeting planner asks you five minutes before you begin speaking if you will permit taping! It's frustrating because you can't win. You say "yes" and it rubs you the wrong way; you say "no" and you're the bad guy.

Try to determine at booking time if this is going to be a possibility, then check all of the factors that will help you make a proper decision then or later. There are several choices.

Some say "Sure, go ahead, record it. More power to you." And if the recording is being done by the audience with personal machines, the recordings will be far below marketable level anyway.

But if the recording is being done by an outsider, a recording firm, or off the sound system, the issue is what they are going to do with the final copies. If they are going to sell them to their members or to the public, and a profit will be made from your labors, I feel that you have a right to some of that profit!

How do you handle that? You can still tell them to go ahead, no problem -- and no money for you. You can give them permission to do it but you want the master tape in 30 days. Or you can tell them that you want $1 per tape produced. As you can imagine, depending on your needs and the volume to be produced, I favor the second and/or the third responses.

How do you know that the actual volume of tapes produced is accurately reported? You don't. (To offset this doubt you might offer a fourth response: a flat fee to have the tapes made which would be up to 50% of your speaking fee.) And if it's a small group to begin with and it sells only 14 tapes, is it worth the negative hassle for $14? But if 1,000 tapes are bought, that additional income is both welcome and deserved.

Think about those approaches and have them in mind should this situation face you. It's best to have a policy established that you can bend to meet specific situations. One way to prewarn the meeting planner is to state clearly on your agreement that your fee does not include taping rights.

A final point: if you already sell tapes, it's best to work a negotiable agreement directly with the client in advance. One way is to give them an extremely favorable price break so your tapes could be included as part of the package to the attendees. (You must work out the use of your name and address on these tapes -- as well as books and workbooks -- with the client or speakers bureau, however, to avoid potential misunderstandings.)

II. OFFICE TOOLS

Communication with the Meeting Planner and/or Bureau

Once we've made a speaking commitment, it is absolutely critical that we keep those responsible for our appearance informed about what we're doing, where we are, and when we will get there. I've had some horrors in this regard -- thank goodness we learn!

On one occasion I was booked for an after-dinner speech on a Saturday evening. I had told the meeting planner that I'd be in town the night before. I would pay for the room for the additional night since I was going to meet with a friend, one I'd had for many, many years and with whom I wanted to relive old times. But at the last minute my friend couldn't come, so I called the hotel and cancelled the reservations for Friday. The problem was that I didn't also call the meeting planner, who still thought I'd be there then.

Mind you, that was 24 hours before the speech, far more than necessary. But I had told the planner that's when I would arrive!

I ended up leaving home on Saturday morning. He called but since I'd already left town, he couldn't reach me. He was so concerned, he actually hired another speaker as a back-up, in case I didn't arrive -- because I hadn't kept him informed on what was happening.

The result? He was upset. That bothered me, and I simply couldn't do the kind of job I wanted. The audience response wasn't good. And I wound up reducing my invoice by the amount he paid the "back-up" speaker, out of guilt.

Now, I try to share any plans and changes in plenty of time so the person booking me is comfortable -- and I am too. The difference is a phone call! I encourage you to do the same: let the meeting planner or speakers bureau know of your travel plans: times, means of travel, hotel/motel accommodations, and anything else concerning the booking that will put their and your minds to rest, so you can focus on the key element, the speaking.

If we're going to be professionals we must take the responsibility for acting professionally. Zig Ziglar says it best: "Every time we point the finger at them, there are three more pointing back at us." We must accept the fact that if there is any communication error that takes place, it is our job to start straightening it out!

Another example is a speaker who booked an engagement almost a year in advance and had written several confirmation letters but never heard anything back. Finally, with two months to go, he decided to phone. The meeting planner wasn't there any longer. They hadn't been forwarding his mail. He was somewhere else. The engagement was off!

In the meantime the speaker had turned down other bookings for that original date. He eventually found the planner at a new location, and he agreed to book him at some future time with the new firm -- but think of the money and time that were lost, beyond the wasted energy, for wont of a simple phone call when he didn't hear back from his first confirmation letter.

Contracts, Agreements, and Invoices

There is no right way. Many speakers have their own agreements or contracts. Almost all speakers bureaus have their own agreement forms for both the speaker and the client. Every bureau has a slightly different approach and those speakers who have their own formal agreements cover different items.

A few thoughts, nonetheless:

(1.) If you are working through a bureau, accommodate yourself to their procedures, even if they are sligtly different from yours. The speaker can be more flexible than a bureau that might have been working with the same client the same way for many years.

(2.) Some speakers merely use a letter of confirmation which outlines the details of the engagement and how the payment will be handled. (I have always billed the client after the speech and have always been paid.) Other speakers ask for half of the fee in advance, with the other half due at the engagement. Some ask for the fee at the engagement, and they bill the client afterwards for expenses. Still others predetermine the expenses and ask for full payment of fee and expenses at the engagement. (If the estimate of expenses is too low, the speaker in this case usually absorbs the difference.)

(3.) If you are using a formal agreement, be sure to call it an "agreement" rather than a "contract." (Contract has a negative connotation.) Some speakers have clauses which call for partial or full payment if a cancellation arises within a certain time period prior to an agreed speech date. (If nothing is paid in advance, this is hard to enforce and usually not worth pursuing. You might consider the practicality of including the clause in that case.)

(4.) Most speakers bureaus ask for a 50% deposit, to protect the speaker and the client. Therefore, should a cancellation occur, the speaker usually receives at least his/her percentage of the deposit.

(5.) Whatever policy you follow, be consistent.

Invoicing the client

It's easier to invoice the client than send a letter/breakdown each time. It can be as simple as the example that follows. Be sure to fill in any areas of concern to the meeting planner.

Odd as it sounds, some speakers don't "get around to" billing until days or weeks after their presentation. In the meantime the client is eager to wrap up the convention, to pay the expenses right away. Or the speakers bureau wants to get the bill sent promptly.

I have to call at least 20% of the speakers we book ten days after the engagement to get their bills! You'd think they'd have it in my hands before the last word stopped echoing. And a few do. But many just take their time -- then want to get paid instantly!

That can cost you future bookings. Don't delay a paying client! Don't dally billing a speakers bureau! Keep current on the paperwork, maintain a file or folder on each engagement, and wrap up each commitment promptly and accurately.

And be fair. If you've got a hotel bill with personal phone calls and extra room service charges on it, bill the client only what he owes. If you pad, someday you will pay the piper. It will come back to haunt you -- which, to speakers, means lost business. Keep your receipts, tally them honestly (even in favor of the client if there's any question), and submit your invoice promptly.

Fees

Once you have passed the vital "freebie" stage, you are faced with determining fees, knowing when to raise them, and what precisely you can add to them to cover costs.

The fee you charge is based on the demand for your services, not on your desire to make money. Therefore, a fee schedule normally starts at a modest rate, say $100 a presentation or less, and moves up as market interest, mainfested by fee paid bookings, continues to demand you at higher rates.

Let's look at a hypothetical fee schedule that assumes the speaker, living in Los Angeles, offers both speeches of an hour or less and longer programs of up to four hours:

INVOICE

Speaker _____

Client _____

Speech date _____

Speech location _____

Speaking fee: (___ hours) $ _____

Airfare: coach (____/____/____)   _____

Hotel/Motel   _____

Rental car (if applicable)   _____

Ground transportation/parking (home)   _____

Ground transportation/parking (site)   _____

Meals   _____

Tips   _____

Printing expenses for handbooks   _____

Cassettes/books/workbooks/manuals   _____

Miscellaneous   _____

                                                 _____

                    TOTAL $ _____

Comments/Explanations:

Please make check payable to: John J. Doe

My tax I.D.# or S.S. # for your records:
                    43-8989898

Send check to: John J. Doe
                 1010 Main St.
                 Anytown, USA 11111

If you have any questions, please call me at:
                    (800) 444-1111

Location of speech	Up to 1 hour fee	1.5-4 hour fee
Greater Los Angeles	$ 600	$ 800
Within driving distance	750	1250+
West of Mississippi River (Air)	1000+	1500+
East of Mississippi River (Air)	1500+	2000+

(+ means "plus expenses)

Such a schedule allows the speaker flexibility in quoting fees based on the length of time that necessary travel will require, even though the actual speaking time remains constant. It makes sense to offer your services for less in your immediate living area, then increase the cost for them progressively the farther you go. The shedule also brings you comfort in knowing exactly what is being quoted to everyone.

The above schedule isn't for everyone. Its rates indicate that the speaker has been successfully booking for a reasonable period of time. If you have no idea where to start your rates, talk to a speakers bureau or somebody knowledgable about and experienced in the speaking trade.

Nor is the schedule totally inflexible. If the client speaks of multiple engagements, for example, be prepared to negotiate. On the other hand, on those rare and delightful times when you are paid "higher than usual" for a particular speech, that is no call to automatically increase the entire schedule. Raising your rates might be considered when you have 25-35 speeches "on the book" at your present fee. Then think of a 10-25% increase.

Jeanne Robertson is a good example. Now one of America's top speakers, she began with hundreds of "freebies" for experience. She graduated to $25, $50, $100, $250, and as recently as six years ago she was earning $500 per speech. In 1984 she has more requests than she can possibly handle at $2500 per speech. (By 1994, who can even guess?)

To those who are unaware of her patiently programmed rise Jeanne Robertson is an "overnight success"! But it took ten years for that night to arrive! She raised her fees because she became a professional/professional, and demand took over from there.

Some speakers charge by the number in attendance. Unless a costly handout is provided, rarely is this practical. Many groups of 25 can afford more than groups of 2,500. Determine fees by the length of the presentation, the location (amount of travel time), and the volume and difficulty of specialized preparation.

Airfares

If you must fly to reach a speaking destination, the client is expected to pay that expense, plus your hotel, ground transportation, meals, and all directly related incidentals, as indicated on the sample invoice.

The two most pressing questions concerning speakers and airfares is whether they can ask for "first class" tickets and how rates are prorated.

Most celebrities fly first class but only recently have the top, non-celebrity speakers begun to make the same request. Their logic is that "to get a first-class speaker they should pay first-class airfare." I disagree with this philosophy.

It's not my role to tell others how to fly nor the class of accommodations they should book, but I fear that newer speakers will be misled by this logic to think that by rights they too should make the same demands -- and thus lose engagements when the clients balk.

I can understand a 6'9", 440-pound speaker making the request. But for the rest, when you fly your family first class on a vacation then it's time to think of such a demand to your client. Remember, many corporations won't even let their executives go first class!

There is an exception, though. When you are heading to an exotic site to speak, you want to bring your spouse along, and the client has agreed to pay for a first-class ticket knowing that you will, in fact, both fly coach, using the fee to partially cover the spouse's flight, graciously accept this rare kindness! But be certain that what you are doing is clearly communicated to the client.

The "first class" issue somehow puts the cart before the horse. When travel costs run many hundreds of dollars, or even a thousand, you should be looking for ways to help the client save money, not spend it. Like "super savers," for example, when they allow you sufficient time on both sides of the engagement. And prorating, soon to be discussed.

Speakers get a bonus just by flying: the frequent flyer premiums, of free trips, automatic upgrading, etc. I doubt whether any speaker is passing these back to the client -- nor do they need to. But increasing the costs to that client seems equally unwise. It's likely to come back and haunt the speaker.

As for **prorating** airfares, this becomes important when you have two or more engagements on the same trip whether or not they are in the same city. You live in Kansas City, for example, and give a speech in Dallas one day, Houston the next. You can either split the airfare in half for each client, since they are nearby, or you can figure the exact amount and percentage each client should pay.

Stick to this premise and you won't go wrong: **it is totally unethical for a speaker to make money on expenses.** You sell two things as a speaker: your presentation and your ethics. Compromise either and you weaken your salability. Strengthen either and you increase your sales.

Play games with expenses and in the long run you lose business -- and nobody tells you why. I've had speakers send me billings for full round-trip airfare when the speaker had another engagement on the way or the way back. I've had speakers charge first class and fly coach. I had a speaker with a $100 room charge for food. I even know of a speaker who sent his speeding ticket to a client because he got it on the way to the speech! These things too return to haunt you.

Inquiry Form

The "inquiry information" form that follows is designed to centralize the most important booking information in one place, rather than on fragments of dinner napkins, the inside covers of your appointments book, and scraps of your handout material.

These are the essentials: you can alter or add to this form to suit your specific needs. It can also be kept by the phone as a checklist of key questions you may ask of a telephone inquirer.

One item deserves special comment. "Contact source" means "how did they hear about me?" It's important so you can see which of your marketing methods, your means of promotion, is working. How do you know if the mailings are bringing positive results unless you ask? If you run a space ad in a magazine, how will you know the number of respondents without asking this question? Only by measuring the number of responses for each marketing method will you be able to see which should be continued, or even expanded, in the future.

You have another reason if you work through speakers bureaus. Often a booking that a bureau arranged will blossom into other bookings, and the bureau properly expects to receive a commission on such "hitchhike" fees. By asking how the potential client heard about you, it will become obvious when you should pay the bureau.

Inquiry Sheet

INQUIRY INFORMATION

Company or Group _____

Address _____

City/State/Zip _____

Phone (_____)_____

Contact Name(s) _____

       Title(s) _____

Date of Meeting _____

Location of Meeting _____

Time of Speech _____

Number of Attendees _____

Contact Source _____

Date of Inquiry _____

FEE QUOTED $_____

CONTRACT OR CONFIRMATION RECEIVED   _____

OTHER IMPORTANT DETAILS:

PAST SPEAKERS:

Answering Machine or an Answering Service

There's nothing more ludicrous than sending out thousands of flyers and then have the respondents call an unanswered telephone!

Most speakers operate out of their homes, and many have other activities that keep them away from their phones much or most of the day. A good answering machine (or a service, if reasonably priced and efficient) is the answer. The cost, from $100-300, will be quickly recovered in the engagements that might otherwise be lost.

People don't like to talk to machines? Right. But they like calling a repeatedly unanswered phone even less. On the tape you tell them to please leave their name and phone number so that you can get back to them. (Sound articulate!) And then you call. It costs money, first for the machine, then for the call. But how do you get people to invest in you if you don't make some investment in them?

Speech Files

A professional/professional has to be organized! Most have a special system for filing all of their pertinent information about each speech so that the details can be recalled, accurately, months or years later.

A few years back, Ira Hayes introduced me to an excellent 9" x 12" manila (or white) envelope on which had been printed such things as expense breakdown, specific information about the client, a checklist of the stories and ideas he used in that speech, etc. Inside he would put all pertinent information that the client had sent him in advance, plus specific items he wanted to retain regarding the client and/or the speech itself. An example of that model follows.

I have modified that to use an envelope 4 3/4" high by 11" wide, since only about 20% of the groups send material which could not be folded to fit inside this envelope. (For that 20% I store their material in 9" x 12" envelopes.) On the top of the envelopes is printed the following so that all past speeches can be filed by client name or by date:

----------------- --------------------- ------
CLIENT NAME   LOCATION OF SPEECH   DATE

Speech File

SPECIAL NOTES	Client: _____

SPECIAL NOTES

Client: _____

Address: _____

City _____ State _____ Zip _____

Contacts: _____
_____
_____
_____

Phone: AC____/_____
       AC____/_____

Type of Meeting: _____
Exact Time Frame: _____
Props Requested? _____
Audience: _____
Notes? _____

Other Info: _____
_____
_____

Outgoing Comm. Log:

___/___ Bio Pix Brochures

___/___ _____
___/___ _____
___/___ _____
___/___ _____
___/___ _____

Agreed on Fee: $_____ _____

Advised Pro-rate? + - _____

TRAVEL PLANS

Arrive: _____ Depart: _____
_____   _____
To Be Met? _____   _____
                          _____

Source of Engagement:

Confirmation?

A Creative Idea From This Trip: _____
_____
_____
_____

TRAVEL EXPENSES

Date:							
Air Trvl:							
Ground Tr:							
Grat:							
Meals/Ent:							
Printing:							
Lodging:							
=							
=							

Explanation: _____
_____
_____

Mailing List Additions:

Meeting Site:
Hotel:
Reservations Made?

Date/ AM AF EV

ORGANIZATION:

This speech file was developed by Ira Hayes. It is a plain white 9" x 12" folder printed on the flat side only, with the opening on the reverse side under the copy reading "Meeting Site: _____" and "Organization."

Incidentally, for any of you who may later apply for the C.S.P. designation from the National Speakers Association, this system will prove invaluable. I know some speakers who spent 50 hours trying to verify the particulars on the 250 engagements necessary to qualify. Can you believe that two of them spoke exclusively on "time management and organization"! This reduces it to a few hours at most.

Reconfirmation of the Time Allotment

As odd as it sounds this can cost you later bookings. When booked it is normally for a designated period of time. Reconfirm this and the engagement some days before the actual booking, then double-check it that day or evening to make sure that the original expectations prevail. Without doing that you have no way of knowing that the programmer, while slotting you for an hour presentation, is getting hopelessly behind schedule and would far prefer you to cut your talk to 45 minutes.

I recently had a speaker contracted for 45 minutes who rambled on for 90. The clients didn't tell him that they were upset, so he didn't know. Since he got a fine ovation from the group, he thought everything was great. But I heard from the meeting planner who was quite annoyed because the extra speaking time threw her off schedule.

Double-booking

A client calls to book you two months from now but you're already scheduled to speak elsewhere.

You could simply tell the person that you're booked that day, you hope they will call again in the future, and hang up. Effective for the moment but not farsighted!

You might say, "Gosh, I'm awfully sorry, I am booked that day but I hope I can speak for you another day, if your schedule is flexible. Or perhaps I could be included in next year's program." That's better. If they are willing to change this year's program date, that's a super compliment to you. Or if they will book you for next year, that's great too. By suggesting alternatives and showing interest, you can often turn a "no" into a delayed "yes."

But if neither of these work, a sensible third choice would be to suggest either another speaker whose topic and/or fee range meet their needs or a speakers bureau that could provide them with professional talent. If they are pleased with your help, even though you couldn't speak in person, they will surely look favorably upon you the next time they need a speaker.

Code of Ethics

The National Speakers Association has a "standards of behavior" that is basically a code of ethics for speakers. I commend it to all readers of this book, whether you are a member of N.S.A. or not. It follows.

STANDARDS FOR PROFESSIONAL SPEAKERS

The Standards of Professional Conduct for members of the National Speakers Association have been adopted by the membership to promote and maintain the highest standards of service and personal conduct. Adherence to these standards is required for membership in NSA to assure public confidence in the integrity of those who speak professionally.

As a member of the National Speakers Association I shall:

1. Fairly and accurately represent my qualifications and experience in both oral and written communications.
2. Expand my talents and abilities without infringing on the rights of others.
3. Keep my appearance, language and actions on a high professional level.
4. Strive to keep myself in the best possible physical, mental and emotional condition for my presentations.
5. Regularly improve and update my material and expand my personal, social and civic awareness.
6. Try to understand client organizations and goals, in advance, in order to best meet their needs.
7. Avoid using other speakers' specific material or titles without giving appropriate credit.
8. Practice what I preach to others; inspiring and motivating them by example.
9. Avoid conflicts of interest.
10. Share my knowledge and experience to encourage and support other members in the development of their skills.
11. Restrict myself to positive, truthful statements when asked to comment on other speakers.
12. Recommend qualified speakers, or agents, when I receive requests for presentations I am unable, or unqualified, to fill.
13. Maintain the trust of clients, agents or other speakers who may reveal confidential information to me.
14. Refuse to work for, support, or lend my name to, organizations which engage in unethical practices.
15. Constantly search for ways to be of greater value to clients, the speaking profession and the National Speakers Association.

Chapter 5

The Speaking Format

I. SPEAKING FORMAT

Using New or Old Speech Material

An argument for never making a change is Ira Hayes. He has been giving the same basic talk for over 20 years, explaining to his listeners, "it's easier for me to get a new audience than to develop a new speech." For him it works because his material is so good that people want to keep hearing it. He doesn't have to keep creating new material.

On the other hand, many of us who offer workshops or branch into new fields do need new material. Which is not to say that we can't incorporate good audience-tested material that worked well in our earlier presentations, just so it is appropriate to the new topic and hasn't already been heard by the new audience.

There is a very real danger in changing material, though. Some of the best speakers in America aren't as good now as they were originally. They think that everybody has already heard them, they change their speech, and the quality drops. So, again, if you have good stories that are well received, think long before substituting for them. Read your evaluations closely, get input from others both inside and outside the speaking profession whose opinions you value, and try to keep a core of solid material around which you can add, change, and modify.

Speaking Too Fast or Too Slow

Evaluations will keep you honest here, though there are times, as the minutes tick faster than our tongues move, when we are all forced into it.

I've noticed something in two top speakers that we might all benefit from knowing: they used to speak at a pleasing pace but now they speak so quickly it's hard to tell what they are saying. The cause is easy to see. As they have become more successful and effective, they have created more material. But the presentation time remained the same! So they are trying to race through too many ideas and words. Deletions are called for -- hopefully of something other than their best material!

Many speakers have a fast-paced style, anyway. That is fine, providing they don't get carried overboard and their evaluations never indicate pacing as a problem.

Previewing Other Speakers

Any time a good speaker comes to your area, try to hear that person speak. Study them. Perhaps they use a technique, a skill, or a tool that you can learn from. Something new and useful in their voice inflection, animation, gestures, humor, or material? Keep growing. No matter how high up the ladder we go, someone else always has something to teach us.

Just as some make it a growth experience to read a book every week or month, I encourage all speakers -- whether they earn $200 or $10,000 per speech -- to try to hear at least one new speaker per month.

Sometimes it's as easy as staying at the very program where you are speaking for another hour or two, to hear your colleagues on the same platform. Rather than catch the flight 45 minutes later, get the one that follows. The others will be flattered that you stayed to hear them. And you will be following a well-trod path: some of the greatest speakers I know wouldn't miss a chance to hear others speak, to learn from them and to help them as an evaluator.

Audio-Visuals

Some speakers use audio-visual materials as part of their presentation. While a whole book could be done on this subject alone, in any session longer than 90 minutes audio-visual aids are probably beneficial to the speaker and the audience. Some speakers use them regardless of the length. And any speaker who uses them effectively will have an upper hand on those who don't.

The most important thing is that they be used right -- appropriately timed and in support of a point made -- and that they look professionally prepared. For example, if you use predone overheads, be sure they are neat, large, and totally readable from any point in your audience. How often have you heard a speaker quote figures, then show the numbers on an overhead -- typed and invisible beyond the third row?

The master of audio visuals is Joel Weldon, C.P.A.E. Try to hear and see him speak. Or buy a two-cassette tape program called "Elephants Don't Bite. It's The Little Things That Get You." It covers dozens of points that those who use, or plan to use, overhead projectors must know. When delivered to the 1981 N.S.A. Convention, it was one of the finest presentations ever made to that group. (Contact National Speakers Association, 4232 N. 12th St., Suite 103, Phoenix, AZ 85014 for further details.) Another master of audio-visual use is Herb True. Try to see him in action.

Introductions

We are responsible for good or bad introductions at least 50% of the time. While it is customary to blame the person making the introduction, the problem is usually that we failed to properly prepare both the statement itself and the introducer.

Some speakers don't care about their introduction. "It doesn't make the speaker," they say, and simply take the platform when the last word is said. Others tell the meeting planner, "Here's my brochure -- use what you want!" And still others tell the person that whatever they say is fine. Three fine ways to get a lousy introduction.

For most speakers the introduction sets the tone and establishes their credentials. They want it done right. So they write the introduction precisely as it is to be given, then ask the introducer, "Here's the introduction. To make it easier on you, would you mind reading it exactly as I have written it?" Then they know -- usually -- what to expect.

It should be typewritten, double-spaced, and in regular writing (like this sentence, in both capital and small letters) since that is far easier to read. Make three copies: one sent with the meeting agreement, another sent the week before the talk, and the third kept in reserve in your pocket. Chances are 80% that the person won't have either of the first two and will need your back-up copy! Keep it to 100 words or so, and make certain it does what you want it to do: tells who you are and why you are there, what you will talk about, sets a mood by its tone, and introduces you to the listeners....

Room Set-Up

Room set-up and the availability of proper tools to give a top-flight speech can be controlled and they directly affect your client's perception of how well you do.

But your reaction to the set-up and tools is even more controllable and will directly affect whether you get booked by that client again!

In most cases if you send a checklist with ample anticipation to the meeting planner and then reconfirm those requests by phone a few days before the engagement, things will be as you want them at speaking time. You will have the right kind of microphone, the necessary audio-visual equipment, the preferred room set-up, and the temperature and lighting as requested.

But not always! The horror stories speakers tell! Sometimes communications break down. Sometimes Murphy's Law is in full force. And sometimes, while the planner was overflowing with good intentions, he or she got to the task after the very last minute....

It's how we react on those latter occasions that make the long-term difference. We can "go through the ceiling" when things aren't just right. Or we can swallow our anger and set to correcting what can be corrected, then fit our presentation into the new, less-than-perfect circumstances.

Flexibility and some empathy for the meeting planner seem to be the most sensible -- really the only -- position. If the facility doesn't have and can't provide the handheld microphone that was requested (well in advance and reconfirmed by phone), then a professional/professional will adapt to the lavalier microphone that is available, either holding it in the hand or attaching it.

It's our willingness and ability to adapt to such situations, once we have done all we can to rectify them, that will distinguish us as professionals and help secure our future bookings. If we fail to adapt, if we are hard to get along with, rest assured that the meeting planner, however culpable for our distress, will hesitate to write the positive testimonial letter no matter how good a speech we give.

I've had several recent speakers ask why nice letters are harder to get lately. It's usually their inadaptability the day of the program. A recent speaker was booked for an after-dinner presentation which was tied into an awards banquet. The speaker became irate because his talk didn't start until almost an hour after the client said he would speak.

All speakers have this happen to them. Of course it's frustrating, yet the client is the one paying the bill. If the speaker has a flight to catch based on the schedule originally given by the client, that is one thing. But in this case, the speaker was staying overnight at the same hotel where the banquet was being held. His lack of adaptability and his attitude not only hurt him with the meeting planner, our bureau will never book him again.

It's your choice how you respond to the conditions at hand. A view to the future requires careful pre-planning and tolerant flexibility at the site.

The "80/20" rule in management also applies to the speaking business. It's said that 80% of the business is done by 20% of the salespeople. It's the same in speaking. It is the 20% who are the most effective as speakers, as marketers, and as being sufficiently adaptable when circumstances are unique.

Going Into the Audience

Sometimes this is possible, when the audience isn't too large, the speaker has a microphone he can ca..y or that has sufficient cord or pick-up, and he isn't tied down to overheads or visuals.

Whether it is done usually depends on the setting, topic, and style. But how it's done creates headaches for seminar producers when the speaker wanders down to row four and plants himself or herself for the rest of the presentation! They want to be close to the people, to be able to say "Hi, Sam, how are things going, good to see you, glad to hear that things went well at your open house in Troy the other day, it's really nice you brought a guest with you."

The problem is row four! The brave souls sitting up front either paid more or got there early to be close. Where are they now? Craning their necks to listen to the speaker's back. For a few seconds, okay. For a quick walk down the side or center aisle, fine. But if the speaker is going to stay at audience level, why not right in front of the front row? That way everybody has a good seat.

Unimportant? Not if you turn off 20 or 30 people. Some will be turned off anyway by things beyond our control. Why add to it with things that are in our power? Everything that makes our presentation better or worse is a marketing tool.

Evaluation Forms for Established Speakers

These were discussed at length in Chapter 3 as they pertained to new speakers. Here we want to reiterate the importance of feedback from your audience at every stage of your speaking career.

Sadly, many speakers rise to the top by using strong, appealing words and ideas. But somewhere they stop using the material that "brung 'em." For a while they can "ride on their names," but if pride stops them from using evaluation forms, they lose track of where they are and what happened. Evaluation forms might prevent this from happening; they might also suggest the cure.

Some speakers move from the kind of evaluation form shown earlier to a smaller, postcard-size form that contains the key evaluation questions as the type of groups they face broadens. These mini forms -- an example appears below -- are easy to carry, fit most

Mini-Evaluation Form for Speakers

Friends: Speech date:_____

Please complete this brief evaluation form for **JOHN DOE.** Either give it to him today or mail it, postage paid, to the address on the rear. Many thanks!

(1.) The speaker was: Great ___ Very Good ___ Okay ___ Poor ___

(2.) On a 1-10 scale (10 highest) he was: ___

(3.) I particularly enjoyed the following:

(4.) I didn't like the following:

(5.) Other comments to help the speaker grow:

Optional

Your Name

Company Name

Street Address

City and State

Zip Code

Area Code Phone

(   )

BUSINESS REPLY CARD
FIRST CLASS PERMIT NO 1

POSTAGE WILL BE PAID BY ADDRESSEE

John Doe
1010 Main Street
Canton, OH 44714

NO POSTAGE
NECESSARY
IF MAILED
IN THE
UNITED STATES

This needn't be done in postcard form. You can ask that they be left at the door after your speech.

Nor must it include the post-paid inscription (see the Post Office for exact dimensions, location, and cost), though that will certainly increase the number returned. You can simply indicate a place for the stamp.

Finally, the name/company/address/phone is optional on the back side of the card. It is nice to have, though, particularly if the comments are favorable.

The most important thing: get evaluations whenever possible. They keep you performing at peak level -- and tell you how to get there if you're not!

audiences, and can either be left after the presentation or mailed later. They are particularly useful at luncheon, keynote, or workshop presentations, but impractical at formal awards banquets.

Again, the purpose of evaluations is to help us speak better. If five people say that we don't smile enough, that's something to work on. If somebody says that we look to the right too much, the comment is probably true and worth attention. If they find that our clothes clash in color or style, that's the kind of frankness we need so we can improve. The more honest and diligent we are in asking for input from the audience, the more honesty we are going to get and the more we are going to grow.

Many years back I showed a film as part of a talk I was giving. The film featured the legendary Dr. Norman Vincent Peale. I commented to the listeners that Dr. Peale had gained his notoriety through his many and widely read books about the "Power of Positive Thinking," as well as through his ministry at New York City's Marble Collegiate Church. On one of the evaluation forms a person said that I had used the word "notoriety" improperly and that I should look it up in a dictionary. I did as the person suggested and, sure enough, I found out that I had it all backward: "notoriety" is supposed to be used in reference to people who are notorious or widely known for their misdeeds rather than their good deeds!

II. OTHER PLATFORMS

Public Programs or Seminars

These offer credibility, can be highly profitable, and are excellent marketing tools for our speaking skills. So, again, while I will tell you how to get included in them in the next chapter, let's see why you want to consider them now.

The credibility comes from the company you keep on the platform and the promotional tools you can display after having spoken at such a program. For example, a few years back I was scheduled to speak between Dr. Murray Banks, Dr. Charles Jarvis, and Dr. Kenneth McFarland. If a client didn't know me, he surely knew one of them! The same when I spoke with Dr. Norman Vincent Peale in Kuala Lumpur, Malaysia. Good names to have linked to yours.

I asked for as many marketing brochures as the producer could spare. At times the producer will simply throw away 1,000! So you can rest assured in every case where I speak at a public seminar, I bring back as much printed material as I can! The point: whether you speak at a motivational rally, a Fred Pryor presentation, or an A.M.A. or S.B.A. or university-sponsored program, get plenty of copies of the marketing brochures.

Further, while I'm not suggesting that you lower your fee to speak at such a program (though the producer may not book you unless you do), remember that the exposure at many public programs is incredible. One of America's most successful speakers, Zig Ziglar, C.P.A.E., owes much of his prominence to just such exposure in the '70's and '80's.

If the producer is solidly based and honest, you have much more to gain than lose by participating in almost any public seminar. That gain may be even greater than at corporate or association meetings. The latter seldom want products sold. Most public seminar producers delight in their sale -- as long as they are asked before and they get part of the profit. Which adds up to a huge financial difference to those who sell many tapes or books.

Let me share an example of how product sales can be profitable for all involved at public seminars. I recently had an excellent speaker reject an offer to appear on two of our public programs where we draw 3,000 people each year and 1,000 for the session he would have been conducting. He said no because be objected to including us, the producers, in the profits of the product sale, even though we brought the audiences and manned the product sale booths.

Simple arithmetic shows how much that decision cost him. On only one of our programs, offering items at $100 per (to simplify our calculations), if he sold to just 10% of the audience he would have grossed $10,000. Deducting, say, $2000 for product cost and splitting the remainder with us (our usual ratio), he would have netted $4,000 in product profit alone -- plus his normal speaking fee. Since we were talking about two programs, that decision cost him a minimum of $8,000 plus speaking fees.

But let's say that speaker got booked with corporations those days -- and that the corporations are two of the few that allow product sales. If he had 50 in each audience and as many as 20% bought a product, his gross would be $2000 for both days, for a net after product cost of $1600, plus speaking fees.

That speaker is quite successful nonetheless, but it appears to me to be a case of nearsightedness that the less well established could scarcely afford. Even more so because that speaker lost the potential of many more bookings in the future, assuming he did his usual excellent job.

The public seminars in question have 300 different organizations formally represented in the audience, including many top corporations in the state. Several speakers have subsequently been booked often, directly or indirectly, as a result of this exposure. While in our case, since we are a speakers bureau, we expect the bookings to go through us, many of those bookings would have been made at the normal fee (less a commission to us) -- plus who knows how much more in product sales.

At the public seminars alone, we have sold as much as $20,000 worth of products at one session. I know of others where $100,000 worth was sold. In all cases the seminar producers shared in the profit. But the long-range gain was the farsighted speakers'.

Beware, though. Many public seminars do lose money, and you want to take precautions that the loss doesn't touch you.

Public seminars are difficult to market, and that is the root of the problem. So you must be careful. What most often happens with unsuccessful seminars is that you are contacted, you set the date aside (turning down subsequent bookings), and a week before you are to speak the program is cancelled for lack of sufficient registration!

It's seldom possible to fill those dates at that short a notice, so you are left without a booking or a fee. Check the producer very carefully. Find out where he or she has staged public seminars before. Ask the previous speakers if the person and venture is reputable and likely to succeed, based on their experience with the group. If the producer is unwilling to give you input on his past speakers, beware! (Feel free to contact me to see if I'm familiar with the producer.)

Another way to protect yourself is to require half of your money in advance. Then if the event folds, you won't feel quite so bad.

Public seminars: high risk, particularly for the producer. But they can be immensely beneficial to speakers, very profitable, and a chance to rub elbows with the very best in the profession.

Personally Promoted Seminars

This applies if you already have at least a three- or four-hour seminar which is solid and audience-tested. You can print a simple (yet professional) flyer about this seminar that you wish to conduct in your hometown or a town nearby, outlining its contents and purpose, such as sales, sales management, personal growth, building self-esteem, etc.

Then when you are in town you can go to the organizations or firms whose employees you fell would be most benefitted and interested in your program. You can either sell them registrations (or tickets) to the seminar or you can offer, free of charge, to give their group an on-site 30-minute preview of what will be offered at the half-day or full-day program in the near future. Not only will management often let you present your preview to its people, sometimes it will also pay part of the registration fee for any of those employees who decide to attend.

One of the most successful speakers in America started this way. He charged $99 for an all-day seminar that also included a full set of tapes of the program. He would book the seminar four times a year in his city, drawing from 50-150 participants each time. It gave him good local exposure and his costs were modest: $200 for the meeting facility, $200 to print the flyer, and about $15 per set of tapes for each attendee.

Simple math shows that with 100 in attendance he netted about $8000 from each session. It gave him a "vehicle" to sell when he wasn't out of town speaking to other clients, and it earned him good money. But you must know something else: when he was in town, he worked eight hours a day seeing clients and trying to make arrangements with local groups to promote his seminar. He wasn't selling himself as a meeting planner, rather he was selling tickets to a coming program. It was very hard work and extremely time-consuming, but it paid off.

I'm certain that other speakers have employed this method. But a word of caution is in order: this kind of program won't work by sending out flyers through mail order or by running a few ads in the local newspaper. That may attract a few participants, but it seldom pays the cost of the advertising alone. The only way that this method truly works is by going out and "selling" it!

Chapter 6

How To Market Yourself

I. HOW TO MARKET YOURSELF

For non-celebrity speakers, 95% of our business will come from our own marketing effort! Our effort, not others'. We must accept that fact, then make the business a reality.

We're not going to hire an agent or somebody to work for us as a secretary/administrator, assistant manager, or any other title who's going to be able to get us 100 engagements, out of the blue, if we can't do it ourselves. The only way that is going to happen is when we can do it ourselves. Then we can train someone else to do what were were already doing on our own.

Nor are we going to get speakers bureaus to book us 50-60 times a year. Nor will ad or travel agencies fill our slate.

A second point is nearly as important: focus your marketing on your own home state. The great speech/book entitled **Acres of Diamonds** implies that if we are going to work and get the business on our own, that business is in our own backyard. That's not to eliminate our marketing elsewhere, but I too believe that there is more business in our home state than we can possibly fill.

Direct Mail

I believe in it. But you need a good brochure for it to make sense. And positive results are directly related to the volume you send and the frequency with which you contact prime markets.

Some speakers see direct mail as sending brochures or public relations material to ten "prospects" a week. Some send 100. And some send 20,000 pieces a year. All are direct mail, but only the greater volume -- a minimum of 5,000 pieces per year -- will get an appreciable number of inquiries.

While you'd like to book a speech for every mailing, the primary purpose of direct mail in the speaking business is institutional. That is, to get people to know who you are.

Realistically, about 60% of the generalized brochures you send out will either never be opened or will be thrown away within minutes of being opened. Another 30% will be thrown away within a few weeks, with the remaining 10% kept. The few acted upon could take weeks, months, or even years.

Most direct mail experts tell us that, even with a tightly-targeted mailing, a 1-5% response rate is good. But in our business a response is just an inquiry. Our booking rate will be far lower yet. Why do it? Because the more institutional advertising we do, the more impressions we are putting in the minds of the meeting planners. The more familiar they will be with our names and what we do.

Whether you have 200 or 2,000 meeting planners and association executives in your home state, target marketing would be to set up and maintain a list of them. One mailing to them will barely tap the surface. It is important that you mail to them on a regular basis, perhaps two or three times a year. Keep them abreast of new information, new testimonial letters, new clients in similar fields. Those same experts confirm that the many more times you mail the same basic type of material to the same people, the better chances you have of getting results.

The best direct mail is followed by a telephone call. Some speakers use a return coupon in their brochure to generate a response. Others even include the offer of a free demo tape or a paperback book if the recipient returns the inquiry coupon.

Some speakers feel that direct mail is a waste of time. Most who use it effectively, though, can show specific examples of speeches they got directly from mailing. I encourage including it as part of your marketing efforts.

Prospecting awareness

This is critically important and is as close at hand as the local and regional newspapers.

Every day you will find newspaper accounts of organizations who brought a speaker to town, who heard a speaker, or who gave a meeting where some facet of public speaking was involved. Be aware that such items are more than simple pieces of news. They are future business!

Jot down the information: group, names and positions noted, kind of presentation, topic of speech, length of session, attendance, setting, anything that will help you frame your own talk should you get booked by them later. Then send some information to that group! And again!

I've found that in the course of a week it's almost impossible not to find four or five prospects every day in my local newspaper.

In fact, any meeting or social function that you attend should produce "prospects" through conversations you have with attendees. And don't forget, if you're at a hotel or convention center, to check the "calendar of events" board for that day to see what other meetings or gatherings are being held. More conversations: more prospects!

Personal contact: phone and in person

If we're going to market ourselves we're going to have to spend plenty of time on the phone, for the 80-20 concept I mentioned earlier is equally as applicable to marketing. Getting speeches will take 80% of our time; giving them will take 20. It's a grim reality.

Why do we call? To get contacts to whom we will send brochures, then follow up later by phone. To find names of groups and meeting planners that don't show up in the white or yellow pages or on other "prospect" lists we have. Not to sell ourselves but to let them know that materials are forthcoming that we hope they will look at. And that we hope there's a place where we can be of value working with their organization.

We must live with the ratio. If I spend all day on the phone and send mail and follow up creatively I still can't expect to deliver more than two or three speeches a week. That's the reality in speaking. Not much of the actual speaking is done from the platform. Most of the words are used just getting there.

Membership in important organizations

It's like anything else. If you put yourself in contact with others who can benefit from your services through memberships in third-party organizations, you're going to get business. It comes from the positioning. (You'll also learn about your prospective audiences better by what you absorb at the meetings and conversations.)

In my case, because my topics fit into their needs, I'm a member of Meeting Planners, International; the Chamber of Commerce; and, of course, the National Speakers Association. In each case they have brought me business. Not because I sought it, but because I was there. Others join the American Society of Training and Development. Seek groups most in need of the kind of speaking you do.

Convention Bureaus

I recommend joining the local convention bureau. Most cities of any size that hold conventions will have one. That keeps you abreast of the meetings that are coming to your town. And while you shouldn't expect a lot of results from it, you will be keeping your name in front of those who continually sponsor or program meetings in your marketing area as well as keeping touch with those coming to your city.

II. WHO CAN BOOK YOU?

Meeting Planner

This all-encompassing title describes the person who ultimately engages you for a speech or workshop. It is a term commonly used in the industry to indicate your contact person for a presentation, whether you contacted them or they contacted you.

Their actual titles within the organization, among dozens, might be Association Executive, Education Director, Human Resources Director, Administrative Assistant, Program Chairperson, Vice President (Sales), Personnel Manager, or even a secretary to one of the above. At a university or college your contact might be the Dean of Extended Education, Director of Continuing Education, Director of Community Services, Director of Student Affairs, Director of Faculty Activities, or one of ten other titles.

Usually the meeting planner makes the decisions and handles the details, but at times you are contacted by a person without that authority. Their boss simply told them to "get a speaker," without stipulating fees or any other details. This is one of the hardships of a speaker's existence, but we all survive it. There seems to be no cure other than your professionalism and forbearance.

Advertising Agencies or Travel Agents

This is similar in operation to the speakers bureaus and lecture agencies. Though booking is a small part of their activities, if their client asks for them to arrange for a speaker, you are working through them and ultimately for the client. I recommend your making contact with them in your local market and agreeing to pay them a commission from your normal fee (just like you would a speakers bureau), providing that the speech is for one of their clients.

Seminar Producers

There are dozens of public seminar producers in America who regularly book speakers for their public programs. In this situation you ordinarily represent the seminar producer, some of whom are private, some work through universities, and others offer programs conducted through governmental agencies. This can be a very lucrative means of exposure, continual work, and cassette and book sales, as well as a solid stepping stone for credibility.

Hotels, Motels, and Resorts

While this is a difficult source to mine for bookings, some speakers have taken the time to build rapport with the owner, general manager, and/or sales manager at such establishments so that when the opportunity arises that the person at the hotel, motel, or resort is asked for a speaker, the rapport pays off with a phone call to you. Be sure they have a supply of your brochures. Offer to pay them a "finder's fee" or a commission.

Speakers bureaus and Lecture Agencies

Speakers rely on bureaus to book "additional" business for them, for rarely can any one bureau book one speaker sufficiently often to make a sizable dent in their own scheduling.

To the new speaker, bureaus seem like a gold mine. They book so many speeches a year. Hook up with enough bureaus and all the speaker would have to do is show up, speak, and get rich! Not true.

But see it from the bureau's side. There are just so many speaking slots to be filled. And many more speakers vying for those slots. Add to that the clients' demands: "Send me someone who will keep 'em laughing for 55 minutes." "Send me Dave Yoho." "Send me a person for a two-day sales training seminar who will get them back to the basics. Nuts-and-bolts." "Send me Dr. Norman Vincent Peale." "Send me an expert on Transactional Analysis." And so on....

About 10% of my bureau's requests are for specific people, so if they're not already booked, that slot is theirs. Another 60-70% are for particular topic areas, so the multitude eager to fill the booking is reduced to a handful. What's left are 10% of the bookings for the rest of the speakers. So I wind up booking many speakers once a year, twice a year, even three or four times a year.

But that is one or four more speeches in that speaker's itinerary, and if each of the dozen or so bureaus in operation do the same, the combined earnings is significant. So neither beginners nor veterans of the stump can afford to blithely dismiss the bureaus altogether.

Speakers Bureaus

Primarily Celebrity

Paul Boghosian
AMERICAN PROGRAM BUREAU
850 Boylston St.
Chestnut Hill, MA 02167

Joan McCormick
JOAN MCCORMICK, INC.
35 Tamarack Rd.
Weston, MA 02193

Robert Keedick
KEEDICK LECTURE BUREAU
521 Fifth Avenue
New York, NY 10017

James Keppler
1825 Eye St., #400
Washington, DC 20006

Bill Leigh/Ardis Leigh
THE LEIGH BUREAU
49-51 State Road
Princeton, NJ 08540

Blanche Ross
ROSS ASSOCIATES
515 Madison Ave., #1225
New York, NY 10022

Carlton Sedgeley
ROYCE CARLETON, INC.
866 United Nations Plaza
New York, NY 10017

Helen Adam
SHOWCASE ASSOCIATES
Benson East, A-200
Jenkintown, PA 19046

"All Speaker" Bureaus

Mike Frank
SPEAKERS UNLIMITED
Box 27225
Columbus, OH 43227

Dr. Dupree Jordan, Jr.
SUCCESS LEADERS SPEAKERS
Box 18737
Atlanta, GA 30326

John Palmer
NATIONAL SPEAKERS BUREAU
222 Wisconsin St.
Lake Forest, IL 60045

Cheryl Miller
SPEAKERS INTERNATIONAL
1015 W. Woodland, #1A
Lake Bluff, IL 60044

Bill Johnson
WESTERN CONNECTION
7502 N. Tenth St.
Phoenix, AZ 85020

Ed Larkin
SPEAKERS GUILD
93 Old King's Highway
Sandwich, MA 02563

Janet LeBrun Cosby
CONFERENCE SPEAKERS INTERNATIONAL
1055 Thomas Jefferson, #300
Washington, DC 20007

Don Walker
HARRY WALKER AGENCY
350 Fifth Avenue
New York, NY 10118

Richard A. Stull
SPEAKERS BUREAU N.W.
11319 8th Ave. NE - 407
Seattle, WA 98125

BURNS SPORTS CELEBRITIES
230 N. Michigan Ave.
Chicago, IL 60601

Keith Morris
SPORTS ILLUSTRATED SPEAKERS BUREAU
1271 Sixth Avenue
New York, NY 10020

Wayne Smith
THE WAYNE SMITH CO.
600 Water St., #201
Washington, DC 20024

Bernard Swain
WASHINGTON SPEAKERS BUREAU
201 N. Fairfax St., #11
Old Town Alexandria, VA 22314

Alan Walker
PROGRAM CORPORATION OF AMERICA
595 W. Hartsdale Ave.
White Plains, NY 10607

Richard Fulton
RICHARD FULTON, INC.
101 W. 57th St., #11C
New York, NY 10019

Warren Burke
MID-WEST PROGRAM SERVICE
5309 Vernon Avenue
Minneapolis, MN 55436

Brad Plumb
PLUMB AND ASSOCIATES
Box 3506
Shawnee, KS 66203

Ben Franklin
ASSOCIATED CLUBS
One Townsite Plaza, #315
Topeka, KS 66603

Fran Slotkin
LECTURE CONSULTANTS
Box 327
Mineola, NY 11501

Candace Brar
CELEBRITY SPEAKERS BUREAU
50 Music Square
Nashville, TN 37203

Temp Berdan
NATIONAL SALES SEMINARS
Box 2007
Buellton, CA 93427

How and when, then, do you contact the bureaus? And how do you work with them to enhance your marketability?

Wait until you have a good video tape demo prepared. You can call before that if you wish, but most won't book you until they've seen you performing on video tape. (As you can tell by earlier comments in this book, I'm happy to answer questions prior to this stage, but I know that many of the others won't.)

Approach bureaus in a fully professional way. Send a complete package with a letter of introduction. The package should include a video tape demo, an audio tape demo, and a dozen or more of your brochures. (One brochure is as useful to them as it is to you: it goes to one person! They need many for the same reason you need many, so they can market you properly.)

The accompanying letter should be humble in tone yet well written and clear: you want to work with them, you feel that there are areas where your presentations might help their clients, you encourage them to preview your tapes and brochure. Let them keep everything you send for their files and use. Don't tell them how great you are -- let your material prove it. Be sure to let them know your fees and your willingness to pay them their commission out of the fees.

If they agree to add you to their roster, then to enhance your marketability -- which they want as much as you! -- you should keep them informed of your activities as well as send them copies of new testimonial letters, new brochures, a book you wrote, your monthly schedule, whatever it is that will help them sell you to others.

How important is the monthly schedule? Ask Patricia Fripp, C.P.A.E. and the 1984 President of N.S.A.

I mentioned sending in a monthly schedule at a meeting some 18 months back and Patricia decided to take me up on it. The very first month that she sent us her schedule we were arranging a program in Honolulu. Her schedule arrived the day we were going to the printer. It said that she was going to be in Hawaii the day after our program! So I called her and asked if she'd like to speak in Honolulu the day before her engagement. She naturally said yes! It cost her 20 cents to mail that schedule. What she made from the speech will pay to mail her schedule monthly to all of the bureaus for the rest of her life!

The schedule needn't give the company name where you will speak or have too many details. Just the date and the city where you are booked. From that the bureaus can often hitchhike engagements for you. It gives them more latitude in working with clients. If someone calls to ask if the bureau has anyone available on the tenth, they can quickly check 20 schedules without having to make individual calls. And if the date is open and you are speaking nearby, that may be your lucky day!

Don't be concerned if your schedule shows only four dates for the next month. Remember, your purpose isn't to show how busy you are, but to show when you have open dates to fill.

Commissions confuse new speakers -- and irritate celebrities! Say you charge $500 for a speech. If you get the booking, you earn $500 plus expenses. But if the bureau gets the booking, you get $375 plus expenses, they get $125 (this varies some from bureau to bureau), and the client still pays the same $500 basic fee.

The latter point is the hardest to explain to celebrities. They say, "I make $5,000. I don't care if you charge $10,000 to get my $5,000, I want that amount." Which would then force the bureaus to charge varying amounts for the same speaker! It's a real bind because the bureaus work hard and spend time and money for the engagement and then they are expected either to do it for nothing or boost the fee out of contention!

When you are booked through a bureau and additional bookings come from that, directly or indirectly, you are expected to pay the bureau those commissions -- or let them go ahead and handle the details on those engagements.

Finally, it's seldom in your best interest to work exclusively with any one bureau. That's fine if you have an exclusive agreement with a marketing director or assistant who is doing much of your leg work, but the only time that would make sense with a bureau is when it could guarantee you a certain amount of income that year -- in writing.

Few bureaus can or will do that. By being represented by many bureaus not only can you draw bookings from each, your being listed in their material gives you ample free exposure. It never hurts to have your name paraded before meeting planners free of charge, if the bureau is reputable.

III. GETTING KNOWN

Name recognition doesn't happen because you wish it to. It's the result of persistent marketing and good speaking.

Who are the best speakers at marketing in this country? Dave Yoho, Don Hutson, Cavett Robert, Patricia Fripp, Keith DeGreen, Charlie Plumb, Bill Coplin, John Lee, and Somers White certainly fall in that category. Almost without exception they earn $100,000 a year in speaking fees. And none are celebrities. They simply speak and market that well. They are examples of speakers who have worked hard at getting themselves known.

So let's continue with marketing by discussing other ways to enhance name recognition among those of importance to speakers: those who do the booking!

Public relations

Every time you appear in print in magazines or even newspapers, every time you appear on television, each interview you give you've added to that exposure that, while not directly measurable in immediate bookings, cumulatively elevates you in the speaking ranks.

Films or Video Reproductions

At times an organization will ask you to participate in making a film or video tape that it will later sell or rent. This has been my good fortune several times. Seldom is the initial production very lucrative, though that is for you to regulate through an agreement at the outset. Where it helps most is as a marketing plus, since speaking engagements can come from those buying and viewing the material. Just make sure that you stipulate how and for how long the group can sell or rent the tape.

A deviation of this is when an organization or corporation wants to tape your presentation and use it in-house. That's more lucrative; all details are worked out by agreement before you speak. You might also consider, in that agreement, being able to use that tape yourself in a marketing situation, or editing that tape and using it for other purposes.

In either case, you giving your presentation on film or video becomes another potentially powerful marketing tool. I have several close friends who have been on speaking tours of Asia, Europe, and Australia, directly attributable to their having agreed to be filmed for nominal revenue.

Magazine Articles

If you know something well enough to talk about it, you know something else in that field well enough to write about. You can take your topic and restate it, you can focus on a specific element of it, or you can relate it to another current topic.

Why not make a list of magazines that your audiences are most likely to read, study them, and write an article similar in style and length to what appears on the best of those magazines? But before you actually write the piece, read Gordon Burgett's **How To Sell 75% of Your Freelance Writing** (P.O. Box 1001, Carpinteria, CA 93013; $10.95

with shipping). He shows you how to query first -- and how to reprint the same article over and over later!

Don't let the writing part scare you off. Articulation in speech is easily translated to the pen. You simply need to know how to study the other articles in that magazine to see how yours should be outlined and written. The rest is making the facts, quotes, and anecdotes work to create an item that is worth reading.

Think of the credibility that brings you, to be in print on the pages that your listeners usually read! You may get paid for the labor, but be sure to include a 20- to 50-word biographical short to be run under your name or at the end of the article. The quality of what you say leads the person to want to hear more good things from you. Many a booking has come directly from such exposure.

Advertising

The key to advertising is to put your best words in front of the most interested eyes -- or those with the greatest need -- and then not expect too much.

John Wannamaker used to say that he knew 50% of all his advertising dollars were wasted, but since he didn't know which half he had to keep spending the same amount! So you must figure which publications or newspapers serve your clientele, then test wisely.

I know that I have, on occasion, advertised in a few magazines. And every year I'd get a speech or two from those ads. The ads cost $100; the speech paid $1,000. If I got that speech I was quite satisfied. The trick is not to expect 10, 12, or 15.

Showcases

The name says all: these are programs where meeting planners gather to hear speakers. Yet there are speakers who are reluctant to participate!

Generally you must pay to appear on showcases, yet if there are 20-100 meeting planners in the audience, only those on the showcase will have a chance to get booked. The key to effective showcase presentation (in the usual 10-20 minutes alloted) is to "be prepared," unique, solid, original, and the best you've ever been. Which comes from practice, practice, practice.

Such presentations lead directly to engagements -- many can show one, two, ten bookings from one such appearance. One of my competitors, Dupree Jordan, from Atlanta, has a showcase every May. I've spoken and received five or six bookings, so what I'm telling you works. But something else is just as important.

You get exposure to other speakers at the showcase. The best example I can think of here concerns Jeanne Robertson at the NSA Convention in 1979. And even though this is not a typical showcase -- it's the real fire, speakers before speakers -- she was at that point speaking at about the $750 level and was still little known among her peers. Then she gave an incredible talk to 600 colleagues.

More important than the dozens or even hundreds of speeches that can be traced to that one showing, she had 600 speakers spreading her name around the country. She was ready for the challenge, she was at her very best, and while she didn't earn a dime that night, her earnings have multiplied ever since.

Showcases are usually less spectacular. But on both accounts -- bookings and exposure to other speakers -- they are well worth the doing.

And a final thought

Regardless of how effectively we use our marketing tools, how well we get ourselves booked, and what others think of us as marketers, one thing remains the same: unless we continually work on being better speakers, better orators, better animators, better sharers of information, all of the marketing in the world will backfire. It will just get us business in the short term. We must have something to say and say it well. That is the key to success for the long term.

The great ones -- Nido Qubein, Zig Ziglar, Joel Weldon, Ira Hayes, Jeanne Robertson, and a score more -- are great because they keep working at becoming greater. They keep working at becoming the best.

Chapter 7

Answers to Specific Questions;
Conclusion

(1.) **For how long must you continue to give a speakers bureau a commission on follow-up engagements that result from earlier bookings?**

My agreement with speakers stipulates a two-year period. If you do a speech for XYZ Company and seven years later they call you for a follow up, there is no commission on the second one. Those cases are easy to see.

The gray area comes from hitchhikes of hitchhikes of hitchhikes, where in the last case, if you ask where the client heard about you, they can't answer or you can't link it to an earlier bureau-booked engagement. That we understand.

What we're finding, though, is that most speakers don't ask the first question -- or if they do, they don't properly follow through on the answer. If the person says that his brother heard you speak at a Kiwanis meeting a few months back in Coshocton, Ohio, it's simple to deduce whether it's a hitchhike. If you booked it yourself, it isn't and no commission is due. But if the bureau booked that Coshoction engagement, you must let them know of the follow-up and they are due their percentage.

(2.) **Should a demo tape, audio or video, be done in front of a live audience?**

Yes. The only time that studio taping is of value in demos is to add extra inserts or to do the editing. Use studio taping to complement or supplement the live presentation.

(3.) What is the range of commissions charged by speakers bureaus?

From 25% to 35%. Most bureaus are in the 25-30% category, with a few at the higher rate. With some "celebrity" bureaus we have found situations where they have charged 50% above the speaker's fee. We don't like that nor do we believe in it.

But you can control that. If your fee is $2,000 and you will be making $1,500, you can insist that the bureau put in writing that they are charging the client $2,000. On my agreements the speaker sees exactly what the client is paying. In 99% of the time that's the same fee they would have paid had they gone directly to the speaker. We like to keep it above board. It's much easier to work that way.

(4.) Should you get a state sales license and charge a tax on the sale of books and tapes?

The answer is simple -- yes. That is the law. Check with the taxing authority where you live to find out how the regulations apply. In most cases you needn't charge tax if the items are sold by mail to residents of other states. Nor to your state when you sell them in another state. When taxes do apply -- when you sell a book or tape to a buyer in your state -- either you add it to the value of the item (say, $10 for the book and 60 cents for the tax, if your state charges 6%, for a total of $10.60) or you deduct it from the $10 and pay the 6% yourself later at collection time. Check the local percentage, of course. Your tax attorney or accountant should be versed on this if the information provided by the state isn't clear. (You don't charge for services, however. There is no tax on delivering a speech, offering a workshop, or consulting.)

(5.) Once the testimonial letters start getting dated, can you tape over or basically "white out" the date?

Yes. No question about it. There gets to be a point where the date starts detracting from the message. Say in ten or twelve years! But it's one of your best letters. Since the person is still alive and would say the same thing again, the only alternative is to obliterate that date and use the letter as is.

(6.) What mileage fee should we charge for expenses?

This varies from person to person. I now charge 22 cents a mile. Others charge 25 cents. Be consistent, though. If you charge one client 22 cents, charge them all the same. When this book is read ten years from now it may be 50 cents!

(7.) At what speed should we professionally record a tape?

From an editing standpoint, 15 ips is best. As for the best tape, I can't suggest a preferred brand name since there are half a dozen good tapes now available. Go to a quality shop in your city and let them guide you.

(8.) At what point, "fee wise," would a bureau be interested in a speaker?

I'm not sure that the fee is the major factor. It's the talk itself and the commitment to speaking made by the speaker that matters.

Some take ten years to prepare a good video tape, an equally good audio tape, and a solid brochure. Others have it done in 90 days. But once that's done the person has made the commitment to what they are doing: they're saying "I'm good now, I've had other people tell me I'm good, I'm not kidding -- I want to speak!"

When the bureau sees that kind of commitment and the necessary tools in selling, and it likes what it sees and hears, the fee isn't a concern. If the bureau thinks you are ready, it's more than willing to book you. In my case, I'm not looking for speakers but I'm always willing to get one that gives me more opportunity with another client. So it's not the fee structure. If a speaker is at the $100 level and we know that he should be charging $750, we'll let him know. We have booked speakers for as low as $300.

(9.) How can we better utilize the testimonial letters once we get them?

We mentioned sending them to individuals or groups when they inquire. But let's say you get a great letter from the Texas Association of Realtors. You can copy that letter (with their permission), add a cover letter, attach a brochure, and send it to every other Association of Realtors in the country. It works with any kind of flagship letter of interest that could be sent to other groups with similar intersts, be they credit unions, corporations, accountants, associations -- any group that pays to hear outside speakers.

(10.) If I have two phones must I get two answering machines?

I don't recommend two. Just publicize one of those numbers as your business phone and use the machine on it only. I have two phones, one to answer incoming business calls (to which the answering device is attached), the other for me to call out or for use by friends who know me personally to call in.

(11.) **What should be on the recording?**

No doubt you, like I, have heard telephone tapes that range from brilliant to embarrassing. Most are somewhere in between. So figure out what you want the caller to hear, write a short script that gives that message, speak with joy and clarity, and make the tape.

Then get a trusted friend or two to listen to that tape by calling you, to both hear the message and the sound. If they like it and you are comfortable with their opinion(s), that is what should be on your recording.

A possible tract might be, "Hi, this is (Mike Frank). I'm terribly sorry I'm not available to take your call. Please don't hang up. I don't like these machines either, but if you'll leave your name, area code, and phone number, I promise I'll call back as soon as possible. Thanks so much for calling. Please leave your message at the sound of the tone."

A regular answering service is a good idea if you can find one that will answer your calls properly. I've had problems in this regard. I've yet to find one in several cities where they would conscientiously answer the phone, take a good message, be polite, not put people on hold, etc., consistently.

(12.) **What's the difference between target marketing and shotgun marketing?**

When you shoot at a target you have one objective in mind; you have narrowed your focus to one pursuit. Shotgun marketing is far less precise: you shoot and see what you hit in the general area.

The latter is sending your brochure nationwide; target marketing is focussing on your state, from your city outward. University extended education programs use a shotgun market. They list 100 seminars in a booklet and send it to 100,000 people, thinking that enough will find what they want to make the offerings a success.

Speakers target market, on the logical assumption that promotion costs money and it makes the most sense to put a brochure in the hands of those most eager to hear a speech or book a workshop about their topic. If your speech is directed at bird conservation societies would you send a brochure to the first 50,000 companies on a random-selection mailing list? That would waste at least 49,999 brochures plus cost a fortune for their mailing, just to find one prospect. Rather, target marketing is finding a list of bird conservation societies, then sending to each a brochure, a cover letter, many testimonials, and a follow-up call later.

Find your "comfort zone," that area where you feel best speaking, where your topic and beliefs are most appropriate and needed. My comfort zone is working with those in small business, because there I can talk about sales, sales management, marketing, recruiting, and training. So my target is the small business, first nearby, then in Ohio, and then elsewhere. Zero in on your market and sell to them. Focus where people most want and need to hear what you have to say.

(13.) **How do you use an evaluation sheet if you are a luncheon or after-dinner speaker?**

It's much more difficult, no question about it, especially if it's a formal function.

Much depends on the size of the group. With 500 it's harder than when you have ten tables of ten people at each. But work this out with the meeting planner. Ask whether you can leave evaluation forms on each table, then either you can refer to them in your speech or the planner can refer to them after you've finished.

How do you explain why you want them? Humbly. You're really saying, "Hey, gang, I love being here but I'm still growing and I need your input."

"I'M STILL GROWING AND I NEED YOUR INPUT."

Isn't that what we're always doing as speakers -- and isn't it really those who hear us speak who can tell us best what we are doing right, where we can improve, and what we're doing that drives them nuts?

About nine years ago a speaker addressed a very unusual group in Denver, Colorado. They were exceptionally successful insurance sales-people. One of the 70 was the top salesman in the country, but the speaker didn't know which one in the room was the "superstar."

The speaker began talking about physical conditioning. As he spoke, in the rear was a gentleman whose face started turning red. He weighed at least 600 pounds. Fat people were skinny compared to him. He was elephantine -- the biggest man you can picture in your mind. While the talk continued his face got redder and redder, until the inevitable happened. He stood up, slammed his hand on the table, and stated ever so menacingly, "STOP! I resent what you're saying. I don't know if you meant it or not but I have taken personal offense to everything you are talking about. I realize that I'm no candidate for any Mr. America award, but at the same time I will challenge anybody in this room to stand up and state that they have earned or produced within one-fifth of what I did last year."

The speaker had just found that company's number one producer!

How did the speaker reply? He said, "First of all I want you to know that I'm nearsighted and I can't really see that far in the back. But even if I could that wouldn't make any difference because my purpose in being here today is **not** to have you compare yourself to anybody else in the room, or in the state, or in the industry.

"My purpose in coming here today was single fold. That was to remind you and everybody else in the room, as well as to keep reminding myself, that we must look at ourselves as we are today in comparison to what we could be tomorrow."

Isn't that the challenge you and I have as speakers? Whether we're yet to give our first speech or have given 4,000, it matters little what has happened up to now or how successful or unsuccessful we've been. What's important is looking at ourselves as we are now in comparison to how we could be tomorrow. Utilizing ideas we've shared, using the input you can get from all kinds of additional sources, understanding that in spite of all that information, and all that input, the most unique sentence in the English language says it all: If we want to be great speakers, if we want to be the best at marketing our services, "If it is to be, it is up to me."

Index

Also available from COMMUNICATION UNLIMITED:

	Qty	Title	Price
BOOKS	_____	Speaking For Money! (paperback)	$ 9.95
	_____	Speaking For Money! (cloth)	12.95
	_____	How To Sell 75% of Your Freelance Writing (paper)	9.95
	_____	How To Sell 75% of Your Freelance Writing (cloth)	12.95
	_____	The Query Book	7.95
	_____	Ten Sales From One Article Idea	7.95
TAPES — SERIES	_____	How To Sell 75% of Your Freelance Writing (4 tapes)	49.95
	_____	Writing Travel Articles That Sell (3 tapes)	39.95
	_____	Writing Comedy Greeting Cards That Sell! (2 tapes)	24.95
	_____	How To Speak or Write an Idea Into a Windfall (3)	39.95
	_____	How To Set Up and Market Your Own Seminar (3 tapes)	39.95
SINGLES		Writing:	
	_____	Finding Ideas For Articles That Sell	9.95
	_____	Research: Finding Facts, Quotes, and Anecdotes	9.95
	_____	How To Write Query Letters That Sell Articles/Books	9.95
		Seminars:	
	_____	Back-of-the-Room Sales	9.95
	_____	Producing and Selling Your Audio Cassettes	9.95
	_____	Mailing Your Product (and Others') by Mail Order	9.95
	_____	Creating, Selling, and Using Your Own Mailing List	9.95

TAX: California residents, add 6% sales tax
SHIPPING: $1, first book, tape, or album;
50¢ each additional, $2.50 maximum

COMMUNICATION UNLIMITED
P.O. Box 1001
Carpinteria, CA 93013